"Tara's work is brave and fresh. H
in her journey so many times.]
could see the common threads of what we change makers are here to do —
remember our truth and shine the love we are into the world unabashedly.
Tara courageously shows us the way and stands as a brilliant champion of her
own and others' light. This is how we heal and serve. Tara, thank you for your
valuable guidance and wisdom. Every woman on the path should read this book."

~ JAIME FLERES, AUTHOR OF *BIRTH YOUR STORY* AND *HONORING
THE WHOLE*

"*Becoming Tara* is a vulnerable story of doing the not-so-easy work of
looking within ourselves to become more of who we truly are. The level of
radical responsibility and self-love Tara possesses is deeply encouraging and
inspirational. This book is a testament to how we can change our world by
healing our wounds."

~ AMANDA JOHNSON, AUTHOR OF *BECOMING ENOUGH* AND
BECOMING FREE

"A powerful journey of self-discovery and transformation. Tara dives deep into
the human experience of concealing our authentic selves, carrying secrets, and
navigating the push-pull between societal expectations and soul's calling. A
profound reminder that the journey to authenticity may be uncomfortable but is
ultimately liberating. *Becoming Tara* offers a beacon of hope for those seeking to
reclaim their true selves and live in alignment with their soul's calling."

~ LYNN MORGAN CARPENTER, INTUITIVE COACH AND
TRANSFORMATIONAL SPEAKER

"Oh my, what a compelling book. Tara has done the inner work to move
through so much that the result is a powerful, healing voice. She doesn't tell her
stories like a sermon on a mount but from a very real, raw, vulnerable place that
we can all relate to. She takes the reader on a journey from a place of marital
discord, people pleasing, body image issues, and low self-esteem and shows how
she fearlessly dove into those shadows to strip away what wasn't needed. What
remains is her essence, shining brightly from every page. And the reminder that
the unconditional love that remains is not only available for all of us but also our
birthright. Thank you, Tara."

~ CAROLYN SCARBOROUGH, WRITING/CREATIVITY COACH AND
WOMEN'S RETREAT LEADER
WWW.CAROLYNSCARBOROUGH.COM

"Being around Tara is like being around Love personified. She literally oozes compassion, healing, and joy out of every fiber of her being. When you pick up this book, you will feel it leap off the pages toward you, enveloping you in a warm embrace and reminding you of the magic that is inside you too! *Becoming Tara* is a book about radical self-love, offering us a blueprint for how to stop the cycle of shame that is wreaking havoc on our lives and showing us how to find the self-love and empowerment we so desperately crave. A must-read for every former religious 'good girl' who wants to build back a trusting connection with themselves."

~ RACHAEL LUND, CO-FOUNDER OF HAPPY WHOLE WAY

"*Becoming Tara* is the beautiful story of a woman born to be a seeker. It is filled with wisdom and intimate revelations. Tara Davis captures the joys, pains, and challenges of courageously surrendering to your personal transformative healing self."

~ KEITH WITT, PH.D., AUTHOR OF *LOVING COMPLETELY* AND *SHADOW LIGHT*

"*Becoming Tara* is an inspirational and insightful guide for anyone who feels called to undertake the sacred journey to self-love and empowerment."

~ M. ROGERS, PSYD

"For thousands of years, people gathered around a fire or in town squares for the healing act of storytelling. Author Tara Davis has harnessed this power in *Becoming Tara*, a memoir, a guide, a transformative force! With unwavering authenticity, wisdom, humor, and so much love, Tara takes you on a journey from loss of self to being fully embodied, demonstrating how to rise up into the person you truly are. This is a must-read for women everywhere!"

~ KRIS FERRARO, INTERNATIONAL ENERGY HEALER AND AUTHOR OF *YOUR DIFFERENCE IS YOUR STRENGTH, MANIFESTING*, AND THE #1 AMAZON BESTSELLER *ENERGY HEALING*

"*Becoming Tara* is a must-read for people grappling with life's challenges, inviting readers to embark on a journey toward understanding. Tara's bravery in confronting her own challenges lights a path for anyone who is struggling. This is a book about authenticity, and whatever you're facing, her journey will resonate with you."

~ T.L. BOWMAN, BOOK ENTHUSIAST

BECOMING
TARA

Begin your own journey!

Tara

Becoming Tara

TARA DAVIS

HOW I FOUND MYSELF AND STEPPED INTO MY GREATNESS

AWAKEN VILLAGE

PRESS

Printed in the United States of America.

Editing by Jaime Fleres
Cover design and interior design by Andrea Gibb

ISBN 978-1-957408-12-5 (paperback)
ISBN 978-1-957408-13-2 (ebook)

Library of Congress Control Number: 2023915664

Published by Awaken Village Press, Sioux Falls, SD

www.awakenvillagepress.com

This book is dedicated to my greatest teachers. Each has gifted me incredible life lessons, both big and subtle.

For Me
For George
For Mom
For Zach
For Mitch
For Ben

CONTENTS

There comes a time when our mission becomes so critical that we can no longer hide. The calling at the deepest part of our being can no longer be still, and we become brave enough to step out of our comfort zone and act on the little whispers we've heard time and time again.

FOREWORD

I met Tara in May of 2016 at her first acupuncture session with me. She was professional but also very laid-back, with a great sense of humor. I remember laughing with her during most of the initial interview that day. From our very first session, I sensed that she was here to do more than just work on minor health concerns and promote wellness. She was ready to start an incredible journey of self-transformation.

At that time, I had no idea I would get to be a part of that journey. Then, as we continued to work together, I saw how Tara worked to heal her physical, mental, emotional, and spiritual aspects of her being. Now, almost seven years later, I see a transformed woman who has the wisdom, insight, and experience to help many other women and men access a higher power within themselves and begin their own journey of self-transformation.

There are many different paths to healing, and no one way

is right or wrong. On her journey, Tara has received guidance from multiple therapists, but ultimately all of her healing has come from within. I watched as she discovered her own ability to heal from this deeper level. And once she mastered this ability to heal from within, she allowed what I like to call the "inner physician" to come forth.

The inner physician is your body's innate awareness or wisdom. It always knows how to heal and in what order to do so. Tara often came to an acupuncture session of ours with shoulder pain or stomach discomfort, but once the session started, her inner physician guided the treatment to a much deeper level. Often the superficial discomfort would resolve because the deeper levels of healing were accessed as well.

As a Doctor of Chinese Medicine, I understand that there are many levels of healing. When there is trauma in the body, there may be different manifestations or symptoms of that trauma. We call these manifestations "branches." The actual experience of the trauma is the root of these branches. Because of Tara's past work in opening her heart and letting go of fear, she has been able to access the deeper levels of healing and reach the root of many of her branches.

Tara's book takes us on a healer's journey. She writes from the depths of her soul as she relates some of the most transformative moments in her life. This book will inspire many readers to reflect on their own paths toward healing. For others, it will give them the courage to look at their healing from another perspective.

We are all here on this planet to experience all that life has to offer us. There are lessons along the way, and those lessons can be great catalysts for personal growth and healing. Tara's book illustrates her growth and transformation as a healer. May this book guide and inspire you toward your own self-transformation.

Namaskaram,

Dr. Joshua Schneider, LAc, DTCM

LOVE LETTER TO MY READER

Soul Family,

You picked up this book today because you asked for a healing. Whether you're aware of it or not, in some way, you asked to be healed and released from the wounding of your past, from the burdens you still carry with you every day. And *your* healing and releasing is the healing and releasing of others. Your healing helps others to heal. We all have stuff to heal. It's part of our journey of being human. It's part of your awakening—the awakening to the life you've known you were meant to lead but haven't quite figured out how to yet.

When I began the leg of my journey you'll read about here, I anchored into the following statement as a compass to navigate what was to come: *When we refuse to look at our shadows, our dark places, we are unable to shine our light. Our light is the most authentic version of who we are.* My soul knew what these words meant even though I didn't know who I'd become as a result of them.

I've always known that I'm here on this planet to help others in a really big way. I've told everyone I've known that I'm here to help the world. But for a long time, I couldn't figure out what that meant. For sure, I knew I was here to help my family, which is the biggest priority of my life. I knew I was here to be a mom, a really good mom. But looking back, I didn't even know how to do that. Looking back, if I had to do it all over again, being a mom would look completely different. But if I had done it differently, I wouldn't have learned the lessons I'm here to learn and wouldn't be the person I am today. I wouldn't realize what I wanted to change. I wanted to show up differently for my kids. I wanted to show up differently for my husband. I wanted to show up differently in my marriage. I wanted different types of relationships than the generations of women before me had known. Thus started my lifelong journey of therapy, healing, and self-discovery.

I know that by me doing me, learning my big lessons, feeling my biggest and buried feelings, healing unhealed trauma and wounds, I was becoming a better mom, a better wife, a better friend, and a better human being. Becoming a better mom meant that my boys were becoming better humans. And their becoming better humans benefited everyone they met. They saw the world differently; they received some kind of healing. And I don't take this lightly. The ripple effect is real. I see that by being the mom and wife I've chosen to become, I'm having an effect not only on those in my family but also on those I can't possibly imagine. But I still knew there was more to what I was supposed to be doing in the world. But what did that look like?

This book is the beginning of my discovering the answer to that question. I've known that my personal lessons and struggles would someday serve others. That through therapy, I was feeling my own pain, shame, and discomfort so deeply that the benefits of this work would somehow ripple out beyond the bounds of my own being.

That time is now. I came here to learn and do and pass it on to you. I agreed before I incarnated that I would experience pain and feel the depth of my feelings so I could open my heart and be vulnerable with you. So you could do the same. As you read through the experiences and wisdom in these chapters, you might recognize your own journey. The experiences, lessons, and depth of my healing came as a catalyst from others, people on my path who have helped me grow. Throughout the book, I'll talk about triggers and mirrors in the form of others, who are our greatest teachers. I believe those who have been triggers and mirrors in my life also agreed before incarnation to be that catalyst for me. To be the ones to push my buttons; to trigger me so hard that I would burst out of my own bubble and grow.

These pages are not about exposing others, my teachers, for their shortcomings or flaws. They are 100 percent about seeing and learning the lessons for myself. The people in my life who have triggered me the most are those who came to teach me the biggest lessons. I am in gratitude every day for the willingness of my parents and my husband to live their lives exactly as they have, such that they've become my most amazing teachers. Had they made different choices and been anything less than themselves with all their wounding and unhealed trauma, I would not have learned the lessons that now grace these pages.

Growth releases pain. It releases unhealed wounds. It allows light into our darkest corners. When we feel the feelings we've stuffed far in the dark, recessed corners of our body, we release the pain body. This is healing. The more pain, shame, guilt, and secrets we hang onto, the more dis-ease and suffering we allow in our body and in our life, the more weighted down we are, and the less room we have for the true feeling and vibration of love in our body. The more we feel and heal, and the more we release, the more space we create to hold the vibration of love. The more we vibrate higher with happiness and joy.

My intention for this book is for your healing: That you will recognize your own wounds and unhealed trauma and be inspired to take your own journey of self-love and healing. That you will gain more compassion for yourself and those you love. That you awaken to your own divine truth. That you expand into the greatness that is you. That you experience greater love, like none you've known before, both for yourself and for those closest to you. That you recognize those in your life who are your greatest teachers. That you know and trust yourself more than you ever have. That you find all the places inside you that hold you back from living a glorious, love-filled life. Once you're able to recognize, heal, and release your pain, the joy and happiness available to you are infinite.

On every flight, the flight attendant announces that all of us must put our own oxygen masks on first before assisting the person next to us. This is what I'm inviting you to do. It's time for you to take care of yourself first instead of worrying about everyone else around you. When you take care of yourself on this deep level, you allow yourself to awaken to the truth of you. And when you have the courage to awaken, you give those around you permission to do the same. We have to take ownership of ourselves and our own awakening! This is the awakening of humanity, and you are part of it.

We came here, to this planet, at this time, on purpose. We are here to learn and to teach, to heal and to grow, and to hold space for others' healing and growth. We are here to love and be the energy of love. There is no mistake you are here. You're supposed to be here. You chose to be here, right now, during the craziest time our planet has ever known, to be of service to yourself and to humanity. You know, at the depths of your being, you are here for a reason. Know that you have led your life completely perfectly up to this point and you'll continue to do it perfectly. Otherwise, you would have done it differently.

I invite you to be curious as you read these pages, wondering what part of the book is meant for you. Be courageous as something speaks to you. Read with complete wonderment.

And when you've squeezed every last nugget out of it, pass it on. I know that everyone who touches this book is meant to have it in their hands. That's part of my knowing: that those who come in contact with these words are the strongest and most courageous of us all and they already know what to do. YOU know what to do.

Know that by being your true authentic self, claiming your birthright, and claiming the reason you're here, you are ultimately, by default, being of service to more humans than you can ever imagine. You are awakening!

I Love You.

*There's a depth in us all where
we know who we are here to be.
We know what we are here to do.*

1

DIMMING

I used to numb out. All the time. I used food. Alcohol. Drugs. Shopping. Sex. Denial. Codependency. Exercise. My kids. Busyness. Anything I could use as a reason not to feel, I did it. I used anything and everything to avoid looking at those parts of myself that made me feel uncomfortable, not good enough, or shame. Because my life was seemingly out of control, I, along with my committed ego, worked overtime trying to maintain control.

My body became a vessel for self-denial and self-loathing. Over the years, what I attempted to keep hidden flowed over into almost every area of my life. I became a hardcore people pleaser, masking my feelings and needs. I let everyone around me tell me who to be, how to look, what to do, how to think, and what to believe. My life was much easier this way. I rarely stood up for myself. I was constantly denying myself. This started at a young age.

Growing up, all the kids around me seemed to tow the party line and behave as they were told. They followed directions, they colored inside the lines, and they didn't question the rules. That wasn't me—initially. In the beginning, I wanted to challenge everything; I didn't want to follow the rules, but this got me into trouble. For as much as I wanted to be liked and be like everyone else, my inner self wouldn't let me. I couldn't do it. I didn't have any judgment toward the kids who were following the rules; I just knew I was different.

As a young girl, I knew there was something great within me. I knew I was here to make changes in a big way. I knew I had intrinsic knowledge and wisdom that I was to impart to others. I knew that I knew things others didn't know. I knew the information I had within me was truth. I just knew what I knew.

In the second grade, I used to do healing work in the girls' bathroom of my Catholic school. There were a couple girls I would always meet in the bathroom. I knew there was something wrong—they were incredibly unhappy. I often told one of the girls that I knew she was experiencing abuse in her house and was so sorry for her. I was relating to her on a level I didn't yet understand. I didn't yet realize my mind had put a previous experience of my own in a dark corner that I didn't have access to. While I was denying this experience within myself, apparently, I could identify it in others. This girl had never said as much to me. It was just a feeling I got whenever I would get close to her. I would hold her hands. I knew that when I held her hands, I could help her get rid of some of the pain. As I held her hands, I had images of her house, the yelling, the screaming, and the hiding of what was happening. I could feel the anxiety, shame, and fear in her body. I also felt the love flowing through my hands into hers and into her body. I knew the energy of love was reminding her of her own innocence and love. It was helping her let go of the pain.

I knew, when I looked into her eyes, she questioned what I was doing. She didn't ask me questions out loud, but I sensed her judgment. She was confused. I knew she felt raw and exposed. For me, what I was doing was natural. I didn't even give it a second thought. It's just what I did. But she didn't understand it. Intuitively, I could feel her shame around what was going on at her house. She felt like it was all her fault. Eventually, I didn't see her in the bathroom as often as I used to. I think she became uncomfortable with what we were doing. It made me question what I was doing. Was this thing I was doing totally weird, or was it what I was supposed to be doing? Being able to tune into people's energy and send them love and healing felt so natural to me, I figured this was why I was here on the planet. Her confusion and denial were planting more seeds of denial for me. It made me doubt my abilities and what I was here on the planet to do. So, I stopped.

At the same time, I knew one of our neighbors had a disease in her body, and I told her as much. She had secrets that were causing disease in her body, and I told her that. She exploded on me and told me I didn't know what I was talking about and to never talk about it again. It scared me. I thought the information was wrong and that *I* was wrong. This experience stopped me in my tracks.

I was learning that speaking the truth—telling others about diseases in their bodies, channeling healing energy from the Universe to help others—might not be the best choice for me. People didn't seem to want my help or to hear what I had to say. Sometimes it made them uncomfortable, like the girls I tried to help in the bathroom; other times, it made them mad and angry, like my neighbor.

From the third grade on, my teachers would tell me to stop talking. I spoke up all the time and had a lot to say. While I was doing my best to refrain from making others uncomfortable, I still wanted to help everyone. I would flit around the classroom, helping other students. The teachers didn't know what to do with me. The easiest thing for them was to tell me to sit down and be quiet. This was the 1970s. Adults were supposed to give the orders, and kids were blindly supposed to follow those orders.

When I didn't follow my teachers' directives or I gave a response to even their rhetorical questions, they saw me as a challenge and a troublemaker. I often felt like the teachers were in competition with me, as if they were mad at me for helping other students by talking through their problems with them. I was confused. It seemed no matter what I did, if I was doing what felt true and natural to me, I was upsetting others.

I knew I was a good student. I knew I was helping my

fellow classmates. I wished my teachers could see I was an asset in school. Unfortunately, even though my grades were great, most of my teachers had written on the back of my report cards: "Tara talks too much. She doesn't stay in her seat during class. She's disruptive."

I felt misunderstood and embarrassed that I'd been called out, that the teachers were tattling on me to my parents. I knew, even as a small grade-school child, that I was here to talk to people and help them. And getting into trouble for that was sending me a different message. How could me doing what I *know* I am here to do be a *bad* thing? How could me being me be wrong? This was always an internal conflict for me. While I was a glowing student with brilliant interpersonal qualities, I felt shame for how my teachers regarded me. And for being who I was. I started to think what I knew to be my truth might actually be just a lie I was telling myself. I started thinking, "Who am I to be here to do big things?" This added to the pile of shame I was accumulating and storing in those dark corners. Little by little, I was dimming my light.

I already felt shame in my body because of experiences I'd had that I unconsciously locked away. I wasn't aware of them on a daily basis, but my body remembered. They were always lurking. I felt like I had a dark secret that wasn't good, but I didn't know what that secret was. All I knew was that it felt wrong to tell anyone, so I kept it hidden in a dark place. Slowly, this secret began to take up more and more real estate in my psyche. I felt shame but wasn't sure exactly what I felt shame about. It made me not want to be fully seen, but I wasn't sure why. I learned early on, for as much as I yearned for love and attention, it wasn't safe to be my bright, authentic, expressive self. When I shined my light, it caught the attention of others and made me vulnerable to others. I thought they might want to take advantage of me, although I wasn't aware of how. I thought they wouldn't like me, they'd make fun of me or try to silence me.

As I got older, my internal battle—with my secrets and shame on one side and my desire to be seen and supportive on the other—fueled every decision and action I made. At any given moment, I teetered between "Don't look at me" and "Please, look at me." On my extroverted days, I would try to garner as much attention as I could get. On days I felt ashamed of myself, I would numb my feelings with whatever I could find. Because my secrets led to a sense of shame and being out of control, I was constantly trying to be *in* control and hide from my gifts. Secrets start to take up space, physically and emotionally. The more secrets and shame we accumulate, the more dark space we create and the less space we have for pure light to shine. And the more shame we have, the more we want to escape feeling it. We find whatever will take away the pain. I was constantly looking for ways to not feel this pain.

Food was the first way I numbed my feelings (as well as my abilities) and remained in control, either by starving or stuffing myself. In my early teen years, I discovered anorexia as a way to stay in control. I would go for long periods of time without eating. I would be so hungry that my belly would burn. That burning felt thrilling because it meant I was in control. I was focused on the hunger rather than the shame. I also discovered bulimia. I would stuff myself. The fuller I became, the less I felt the shame of my secrets. I traded one shame for another. I was literally filling the darkness with food, continuing to add to the heap of what was already there. It was a momentary exit from my reality. Starving or being stuffed gave me something else to focus on other than the shadows within.

In high school, I tried to sleep with as many guys as I could. It was another way to get attention and fill the void that the darkness was creating. Because I couldn't feel it for myself, I was looking for love in anyone I could find. Sex was a perfect escape for me. It was a quick fix of love, or so I thought. Now, as an adult who's been through years and years of therapy, I know what I was looking for. I was trying to fill an unfillable space that had been taken from me. I was also craving unconditional love and attention. I was craving male attention and a relationship with the masculine that I wasn't getting at home. This was another pain I wasn't aware of. Sex seemed like the way to numb it. In a very convoluted way, because of the shameful secret I had, I thought that if I could have a say-so in sex with a guy, he would love me and I would feel better. I wouldn't have to feel the pain of not being good enough or believing my true self was unlovable. Problem solved. Except it wasn't.

When we went to church on Sunday, I felt the shame the

church taught me about having premarital sex. It was preached all the time. I was a sinner. My attempt to heal my shame just added more to the pile. The church also told me to confess my sins. This just led to more confusion. How could I be forgiven? I knew that when I went to confession, I could never admit to having sex because then, instead of being absolved of my sins, I'd be shamed for them.

I was fast learning that keeping my mouth shut was undoubtedly the safest and least painful route to take through life. Over the years, I shut down and dimmed my light. I became the person everyone else told me I should be. I stopped speaking up for myself. I let others walk all over me; they told me what to do, and I did it. I let them tell me (either explicitly or through their actions) who I should be, what I should wear, how I should act, and what I should say.

I was constantly trying to hide from the real me. Deep within, I knew who I really was, but she wasn't the person I wanted out in the world. I'd buried her somewhere so deep that I almost couldn't find her. Occasionally I'd have a glimmer that the real me was powerful and here to do big things. I'd see her and, for a second or two, dream about the girl who came here with incredible gifts to share with the world—the girl who wasn't afraid of being bright and sparkly, the girl who was supposed to help others heal their hearts. But the thoughts of my own bigness scared me, so I pushed her right back into the deep darkness.

When we aren't living in alignment with who we came here

to be, when we stuff our truest selves back in the dark corner, life becomes challenging, our desires get watered down, and we all of a sudden wake up and wonder how we got so off track. We become confused. We get angry. We numb out. We're bitter at the world. We become sarcastic and cynical with everyone. We starve ourselves to be seen. We eat more than our body needs so we don't have to feel the pain of our secrets and shame. We use substances, relationships, media, busyness, and over-commitments to distract ourselves from the pain of not being our true selves.

The secrets I carried, that were buried deep within my psyche, kept me in a cycle of hiding. There was a dullness to me that wasn't my original state. Even though my conscious mind didn't remember them, my secrets kept me from being the bright, loving, joy-filled human I came here to be—until I decided I was ready to look inward.

There comes a time when our mission becomes so critical that we can no longer hide. The calling at the deepest part of our being can no longer be still, and we become brave enough to step out of our comfort zone and act on the little whispers we've heard time and time again. You know the little whispers I'm talking about. The ones you've been trying to suppress your whole life. The thoughts that you think can't possibly be right. The whispers that keep telling you how strong you are and how worthy you are of everything you desire. Yet, you deny them.

When we try to be our authentic selves, not only does it feel uncomfortable to us, but it can trigger those nearest to us who've also stuffed down their authentic self, whether they know it or not. If we fully live out our mission, loud and proud, it does one of two things: it either gives everyone around us permission to do the same, and they start getting brave and allowing their truest self to emerge, or it scares the shit out of them, and they become triggered, tell us to stop, withdraw, and shut us down. In the latter case, it's too painful for them to see us because it's a reminder that they aren't fulfilling their mission and have dimmed their own light.

In my 30s, I started therapy. I began looking at my shadows, the dark places where I kept all my secrets hidden. And by the time I turned 40, I started coming out of hiding. I began learning more about hands-on healing, the gift I used naturally as a young child but had shut down. Now I was ready to see what my gifts were all about. We lived in Austin, Texas, at the time, and Austin is a hotbed of holistic people and healers. I was exposed to ideas and concepts that I'd never heard of. It was the biggest spiritual growth period of my life. My mind was expanded in all kinds of directions. I took classes. I attended workshops. I went on retreats.

When you sign up with the Universe to learn more about yourself, everything that gets put in your path is a learning opportunity. People that came into my life at that time were big teachers for me. I learned so much about myself. The more I re-learned, the more I wanted to learn. And I say re-learned because my body and my soul already knew this information; it was conscious me that had to relearn it again.

One gift I realized I had was the ability to connect with people who had passed on. I could communicate with them and receive messages for those they were here to talk with. I began receiving intuitive psychic messages for people. I also found that I could manipulate energy and direct it through the body, depending on what was going on with each specific person I encountered. I could see and feel blocked energy in the body and guide the energy to release and move out of the body.

Remembering my gifts and practicing them on a regular basis reminded me how fulfilling and rewarding it was. I felt like I was beginning to serve my purpose again. I realized it was time for me to start practicing all the modalities I'd been learning. And what better way to practice than to invite my neighbors over for free sessions. Most of them were willing participants in my practice as I gained more confidence in my gifts. As I continued to practice, I learned that one of my neighbors was in the hospital and had some issues the doctors couldn't figure out. I felt the call to go to the hospital and do healing work with him. But the thought of showing up in his hospital room scared me tremendously. He wasn't one of the neighbors who actually knew what I'd been doing. What would he think? What if he laughed at me and thought I was a quack? He and I were friends, but not that close.

As I considered going to do this work, the memories of past lives flooded my mind. I have clear memories of being a shaman in a past life and practicing shamanic healing, but I did it in secrecy. I didn't feel safe in that life to practice in public. Even if you aren't familiar with past lives, I believe we all have them. You know when we have fears and we can't point to why? Like being afraid of water or heights, but nothing in this lifetime points to having these fears? It's probably a past life where we've drowned or fallen from an enormous height. Or when we have intrinsic knowledge of how to do a task without being taught? It's probably because we've done it in a past life. Or when we just know we have to have a certain career, we've probably done that before. Or when you meet someone for the first time and you just feel like you've known them forever? Probably a past life.

In another past life, I owned a healing shop. It was located in a back alleyway with only a symbol on the door telling those in the know that this was my shop. Going to work, I wore a long black cloak with a hood to cover my face. I had to remain in the shadows. Visitors to the store would come for healing work, buy books, listen to lectures from other healers, and buy healing tinctures. It was like any metaphysical bookstore you'd find today. Except, in this particular lifetime, it was illegal, and I was probably considered a witch. I only practiced with selected individuals for my own safety.

When I started having memories of these past lives, I sought out a practitioner who did past life regression therapy to see what else was there. During one of our sessions, I went into a trance-like state and immediately felt and saw myself in Puritan times. I was in a one-room courthouse. I smelled the mold in the air. I heard the floorboards creaking as the magistrate walked back and forth, trying his case against my best friend. She was being tried for practicing and teaching homeopathic ways of living. She and I worked together, but I sat invisible in the crowd. The audience started yelling that she was a witch. They eventually decided she was evil, was practicing witchcraft, and sentenced her to hang. I knew I had to leave or potentially face the same fate.

Past lives stay with us. It's part of who we are, even though we don't consciously remember it. Still considering whether or not to go to the hospital, I suddenly felt as if someone was pushing me into the garage to get into my car and go. This was a force behind me that I hadn't experienced until that point. So I went.

I easily found his room, took a deep breath, and opened the door. He was definitely surprised to see me. I told him that I had been practicing hands-on healing work with some of our other neighbors and I really wanted to try with him. He said he was totally open to it, which surprised me. He didn't seem like a person who would be into energetic healing. He seemed like someone who needed more concrete evidence. I asked him a couple questions about what was going on, and he gave me a brief description. There was a blockage in his intestines, and the doctors hadn't found the culprit.

As soon as I laid my hands on the left side of his body, heat and energy flowed through them. I stayed there and allowed the energy to do its work. He told me it felt like my hands were warm stones being laid on his belly and that the energy felt really good in his body. He reported feeling such a sense of calm and safety that he wanted to stay in that place forever. Eventually, I felt the energy begin to wane. I thanked him for letting me practice with him and told him I hoped it helped. He was extremely grateful that I'd come to see him.

Later that night, I heard from his wife that things started shifting as soon as I'd left, and they thought he would be home the next day. Funny though, when I spoke with him several days later about the experience, he chalked up the movement in his intestines to the medicine he'd later been given. I chalked it up to his body allowing the energy in and his body doing the work itself. Either way, it was a big turning point for me. It was the exact same thing I'd done decades before as a grade-school child. I could have allowed his dismissal of my gifts to once again shut me down, but I didn't. I knew I was becoming strong enough that it didn't matter to me what someone else thought. I knew I had to do what I am here to do. I felt the call. I acted on it.

Now, let me be really clear: the energy that flows through anyone who does hands-on healing is the energy of the Divine, of God, of the Creator, of Source. I am just the conduit who listens and allows the energy to flow. It's not me personally doing the work. I'm the vessel who allows it to flow through. God is the one delivering the energy and the healing.

We are all born knowing what we're here to do. We intrinsically know the mission we came here to fulfill. But, for a lot of us, that guiding light gets covered up along the way. We forget. We're made fun of one too many times, and we decide being us isn't worth it. So, we shut down that part of us. We stuff it away. We stop being our authentic selves and start being who everyone around us thinks we should be. We become a version that is easier to handle. A version that doesn't rock the boat. A version that keeps us safe and those around us comfortable.

Certain moments in our lives present us with choices—going to the hospital, hiring a therapist, saying the thing, quitting the job. These are critical moments when we can no longer hide and when we choose to start being the humans we were meant to be. They are the moments we choose to look at our dark places, the places where we've kept all our secrets and shame hidden, and become uncomfortable in our own growth.

As we take baby steps forward, we realize we *are* strong. We see that with each little step we take, we *can* do this. Moving forward in discomfort might be the most we have ever done for ourselves. We might decide to finally claim our gifts and start a business despite what others think. Or we might decide to start speaking up and share our truth in our family even though the dynamics will drastically change. Change means something will be different. We're changing our trajectory. And different probably means uncomfortable. But with each step forward, we start to know who we are and how strong we really are. Each step forward creates our own awakening. We choose to allow the truth of who we are to become louder than the numbing we've used to keep it quiet.

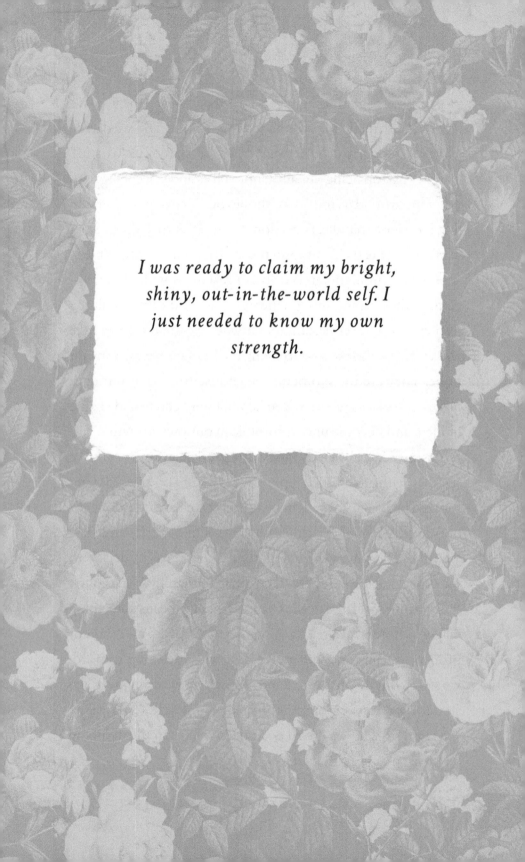

I was ready to claim my bright, shiny, out-in-the-world self. I just needed to know my own strength.

2

REMEMBERING

In kindergarten, my dad made me a stage out of cinder blocks and plywood. It was 1973, and I remember this version of me so vividly. I have a picture of me with a head full of soft blond curls and big green eyes. I wore lavender corduroy bell-bottom jeans and a yellow striped shirt. I was the paragon of early '70s fashion. My dad hooked up his microphone to the reel-to-reels, I climbed up on the stage, took the mic, and talked, and even sang, to my captive audience of two: my mom and younger brother. I would sing at the top of my lungs. I walked back and forth on my glorious platform and did what I knew I was here to do: speak truth to the masses. Just writing these words brings tears to my eyes and sends shivers down my spine, which is confirmation I am in my truth. I know it's what I'm here to do.

This inner knowing of truth has been with me my entire life. Even though I wasn't sure exactly what it meant, I've held it in a sacred place. I've wondered how this would manifest. I've been curious about what my life would look like where I would be holding a microphone and speaking to people. Throughout my life, situations and experiences have presented themself to me, and I've known that each one was a piece to my bigger puzzle.

In 2007, my sisters and I went on a long weekend retreat in the mountains. During the retreat, we each scheduled spa treatments for ourselves. As I sat in the main room awaiting my turn, an oversized book caught my attention. I wondered who this beautiful young woman was who adorned the entire cover of the book. Her skin was emerald green, and she sat on a lotus throne with her left hand holding a blue lotus and her right foot stretched out. Flipping through the thick pages, I read these words from a Bodhisattva Prayer with the Green Tara incantation: "Through the practice of giving and the other Perfections, may I reach full enlightenment in order to be of benefit for all living beings. Om Tare Tuttare Ture Soha!" I was intrigued because she and I shared the same name with the same spelling.

As I continued flipping through the pages, I discovered there were 21 manifestations of Tara—21 different colors, each representing a specific liberation. These were liberations from fear, from poverty, from illness, from suffering, and so on. Overall, Tara represents wisdom, compassion, and liberation. She helps us overcome fear and remain fully present during the difficulties of our lives. She connects us back to our nature of the Divine Feminine. While the teachings in the book seemed interesting to me, I put the book down and didn't think about her any further. It was my first initiation to Tara.

Years later, my husband gave me a statue of the Goddess Tara for my birthday. I loved it. He has a knack for giving me gifts that I don't usually ask for but often become entirely significant to me over time. It's as if his Higher Self knows what gifts to give and when to give them to me. He sees me when I often don't see myself. There is a flow to us that I've learned to trust. I know we've had hundreds, if not thousands, of lifetimes together. I was surprised and curious that she popped back into my life again through him. I knew there must be a clear reason she was back, and I knew I was meant to have her near me. I sat her in my office where I could see her constantly. I remember looking up information about her and learning a few more things about who she was and what her purpose was but, again, didn't feel any sort of calling to meditate with her or learn more beyond what I'd already done. It felt enough to have her sit with me in my office, just being in my space. I didn't need to know anymore. This was my second initiation.

She entered my life for a third time in 2020 after we moved into our new house. You know how things pop into your life and you can't remember how they did or why, they just did? That's how it happened this time with Tara. I can't remember how I came across Rachael Wooten and her new book, but as soon as I saw the title, *Tara: The Liberating Power of the Female Buddha: 22 Meditations to Heal Ourselves and Repair Our World*, I knew it was time to dive in and learn more. I didn't know what I needed to learn or what I was being called to do with it; I just knew it was time and bought the book.

When it came in the mail, I was excited to see not only a beautiful book but also a bonus card deck that came with it. Each card featured a different color based on the various liberations of Tara. The artwork and colors immediately reminded me of the first book I found at the retreat center in the mountains. I was super curious to learn more about what all this meant. My energy was quite amped up, and I knew there was way more to this next phase of my journey than I could put my finger on. For reasons I didn't yet know, this inner calling was telling me it was time to learn more about this Goddess who first appeared in my life almost 15 years before. It was time to sink into her energy and find out why she kept coming into my life.

I had placed my Tara statue in a nook of her own on my office bookshelf. I surrounded her with crystals, a card of Green Tara, a small vase with a flower, small hanging bells with the image of Ganesh (he is the remover of all obstacles), and my picture of me with my microphone as a little girl. I craved sitting in this new space meditating every morning with candles and flowers. I would take my statue of her and place it on the floor in front of me. The book taught me to chant particular mantras, and I loved chanting the new songs to Tara. I used mala beads, and I loved the feel of them sliding through my fingers. I loved the smell of the incense I burned. I loved the feel of bliss I felt when the whole process was complete. And when I finished, I would sit in the peaceful state I'd created in silence, listening to the echoes of my voice still hanging in the room. There was something so powerful in that still peace and in knowing that I had created it—that I had it within me to create my own powerful place of stillness.

During one meditation, the thought came to me that my office was my womb; it was a place of sacredness for me, which I loved. I thought, *if my office is a womb for me, what am I birthing?* I let that thought hang out for a while and marinate without the need to answer it. I knew it would be answered when the time was right. Most of the time, events show up in my life when I least expect them. I pray, meditate, ask for what I'd like, then I let it go. It's taken me a long time to realize that I'm in charge of the asking. I'm NOT in charge of how or when it shows up. That's up to the Universe. The Universe and my Higher Self know exactly when the perfect time is to bring to me what I've asked for, and not a second before.

For months in meditation, I'd continued chanting different mantras to the Goddess Tara. There's Red Swift and Courageous Tara, Great White soothing Tara, Black Tara who destroys all negativities, and Orange poverty-removing Tara. There are 22 meditations available, but I didn't feel called to use them all. Sometimes I didn't know why I was being called to use specific ones; I just knew I needed to.

The emanation I resonated with the most is Green Tara. Green Tara is the essence of pure love. She is here to liberate us from our own suffering. She is known as the Great Mother, the Giver of All Realizations, and the liberator. She helps us realize our own true nature, which is exactly the same as hers. She is the Awakened One. In both Hinduism and Buddhism, she is seen as the female Buddha.

I would sit in meditation with her energy and pray to her, chanting, asking for my own liberation from suffering. And even though I didn't allow myself to consciously know why, I knew on some deep level that I was asking for something greater than my mind could conceive of at the time. I did know I was asking for liberation from my own shackles. I wanted to speak up for myself even more. I wanted to be heard and validated more. I wanted to know myself more deeply. I wanted to know I could trust myself. I wanted to know I had my back. I wanted to be more in tune with my mission. I wanted to see more clearly how I was meant to help humanity. I wanted to be free from whatever fears, doubts, or worries I still had about being seen or any other deep wounds that I hadn't yet healed but were ready to be healed.

And I was terrified. I was praying for wisdom because I knew there was another purpose for my life that I wasn't currently serving, a purpose far bigger than anything I could imagine. I had no clue at the time what that purpose looked like, I just knew this was the way forward. Whatever was blocking me from serving my big purpose, I thought she could help me uncover it. I honestly didn't know exactly what I was asking for, just that I knew it was time for me to work with her. I knew I was the only one holding myself back. I was in my own way, and she was going to help me.

At the time I was practicing my chanting and meditation with Tara, I didn't realize the extent to which I didn't know myself. Before moving to Colorado, I had done work with a therapist who helped me see an unwritten rule that I'd been subscribing to since early childhood: don't outshine those around me and don't speak up and say something different. She is the one who helped me to see how I'd played small in my life, kept quiet, and stopped talking so much. Prior, I had no idea I was making myself smaller, sometimes almost invisible. She helped me see that I continued this pattern when I married my husband. As soon as we got married, he went into the military, and I easily slipped into a similar unspoken rule in the military: don't outshine your soldier. No one told me this; I just felt it. I could be really helpful and take charge of different committees. I served on several boards. I was in charge of our Family Readiness Group of hundreds of women, and I was good at it. As long as I kept my light from shining more than his, everything was fine.

After behaving like this year after year, it became habitual and second nature. I knew I could be cheery and happy, but anything more than that was just too much. It could mean I was uncontrollable. I thought it was only because of the repressive environment of the military (and it being made up primarily of men) that I felt this way. But I realized I didn't want to outshine my husband. There was an invisible line I knew I couldn't cross. This program was running in the back of my mind and was completely subconscious. I didn't even have to think about it. Kind of like breathing: we don't really give it too much thought until we have to. Occasionally, I'd think about how I kept myself tempered, but it was such a triggering thought for me that I sent it right back to the depths from where it came. For as happy as I was, I didn't realize just how hard I was trying to be someone else.

Several years later, during a session with another therapist, we started to unpack this even more. Why was I still scared to be fully me? We explored the deep wounds that I'd been holding onto and why I was still holding onto them and what purpose they were serving. Our personal suffering can take on more forms than we can imagine. When we're suffering, sometimes we don't even realize we are. We might just think, *this is my life and I better make the most of it.* We might think anxiety runs in the family and that's just my lot in life. Or we'll never have a happy relationship because that's how it is. Or that our food allergies are just normal for our bodies and we'll always have to know exactly what's in the food we eat. We don't even realize we're suffering and that we can stop our suffering, that we have an actual say-so in our lives. Or, maybe change is too scary for us. One of my major wounds was not knowing who I really was, and I think most of us suffer from that.

As I look back on my dedicated time with Goddess Tara, I realize my intuition was pushing me to commit to a practice with her every day for a reason. The more I did it, the more

I craved it. When we commit to a practice, any practice, we expect results. Our practice can be spiritual, like meditation or prayer; physical, like exercise; or mental, like learning. And when we commit, it means something will be different on the other side. I was expecting something out of this practice; I just didn't know what. I didn't know what the action was or what I was supposed to be doing. I just thought she might be a good start. So I dove in. I committed.

The words of the Green Tara mantra I chant are "Om Tare Tutarre Ture Soha!" This translates from the original Sanskrit as:

Om, the sound and vibration of pure enlightened consciousness

Tare, the Liberator, swift and courageous

Tutarre, removes all fear

Ture, bestows all benefits

Soha, So be it! Let it be so!

During each round of chanting, I was holding the vibration of pure enlightened consciousness while praising the Goddess Tara and asking her, the Liberator, for swift and courageous action to remove fear and bestow all benefits. So be it! Let it be so!

While my human self wasn't entirely sure what I needed, my Higher Self knew why I called in Tara for the third time—I was feeling the pull to start being out in the world. I was ready to claim my bright, shiny, out-in-the-world self. I just needed some deconditioning, some unlearning, and some guidance.

I needed to know my own strength. When I started on my adult road of self-discovery, I'd occasionally see psychics, astrologers, palm readers, and different kinds of healers, and they would all inevitably weave in the same theme: "You're here to help the world. You're here to be of service to humanity. Your life purpose is that of a powerful, influential leader. You'll be in the world spotlight. You are here to help others heal all over the world." Having had this inner knowing all my life, it felt like it was time to take action. Something told me Tara was the gateway.

As I sat in my office in a normal meditation and chanting session with Tara one day, a movie began to play out in my mind's eye. I saw myself back at our garage in the apartment we had rented before moving into our house. I was standing on the concrete facing the garage and the door began opening up. As it opened, I realized all the belongings we'd stored there were gone. There was dirt and debris on the floor. The garage light was off, and I noticed I made no attempt to turn it on. I was just standing in front of the dark, dirty, empty garage space looking in.

As soon as the garage door completely opened, a rat came forward to greet me. In my mind's eye movie, I was telepathically speaking to the rat. He scampered out of the garage and ran toward me like he'd been expecting me. He sat next to me on my right side and gave me a message, "She's coming!" He was incredibly excited about this event. He said over and over, "She's coming! She's coming!"

He scampered back to the inside of the garage, grabbed a broom, and began to hurriedly sweep the garage floor until it was clean. When he finished sweeping, he hosed down the garage floor until there were no longer any remnants of dirt and debris left. He tossed the hose aside and brought in a floor buffer. He buffed the entire garage floor until it sparkled.

I asked him who was coming, and he told me in such an excited voice, "SHE is! SHE is coming!" His attention to what he was doing and his excitement was palpable. Even in my meditative state, I could feel myself getting excited. Who was this SHE that was coming? I thought she must be pretty important to him if he was putting this much effort into cleaning the garage. I was watching with anticipation.

When he was finally satisfied the floor was clean and sparkly enough, he brought in wood, a hammer, nails, and a few other supplies. In his hurried rat fashion, he began making a platform in the back left corner of the garage. He was diligent about getting it just right. He measured, cut, hammered, and put the wood in place.

When he finished the platform, he began building a box. He had this same hurried, rushed energy about him as he fashioned a box to go on top of the platform. When he finally finished the box, he installed sconce lighting on the walls around the box. The lights pointed up so the lighting would shine upward, not directly on the box. I could sense he wanted the lighting to be just right. It was just meant to highlight the space. As soon as he finished the box, he picked it up and cleaned underneath it. He cleaned away all the debris he'd just created and made sure the space was once again spotless.

When he'd finished his work, he scampered quickly back to me and sat on the ground to my right side, just as he did when we met. "This is all we're going to do for today. She'll be here tomorrow," he told me. And my meditation was over just like that. I wanted to know who and what he was talking about. I had no idea if or when it was going to happen and felt disappointed that I had to wait.

The following day, I had an appointment with the therapist I'd been seeing. I'd seen her several times and really liked her. She had a great vibe and was deeply spiritual like me. I thought it would be fun to tell her about the meditation I'd had the previous day and how vivid it was and how important it felt. She was just as curious about who was coming. She suggested I go back into meditation and see if it was ready to reveal more. I was game.

She grabbed one of her Tibetan Singing bowls and began to run the mallet around the edge of it. I closed my eyes and the sound of the bowl catapulted me right back into the same meditative space I'd been in the day before. It was easy getting there. I was standing in front of the open garage door with the rat at my right side.

As he and I looked inside, I saw that the box he built was glowing. Actually, the whole corner of the garage was glowing a golden white. The rat was elated. He was beyond excited. He started telling me again, with even more excitement than the day before, "She's coming! She's coming!" He could barely contain his excitement. Then I watched him gain his composure and scamper over to the box. He climbed up to the top and opened the lid. The glow coming out of the box was so intense I couldn't see what was going on. I found myself anxious because I couldn't see. I desperately wanted to know what was happening, but all I could see was the white light.

As I watched the light beaming out of the box, I realized there was a figure standing next to the box. I was curious and also completely at ease. There was something extremely comfortable and familiar in what was unfolding in front of me. I could feel the feminine energy of the figure coming toward me. I saw her come to the edge of the garage. The rat was on her right. As the being emerged from the light, I immediately knew it was the Goddess Tara. Something happened to me in that moment. As deeply as I knew this was the Goddess, I also knew this Goddess was me. I was this Goddess. I was her. I was the one who had just emerged out of the box. I was the Goddess Tara. I AM the Goddess Tara.

As I took this information in, I walked toward her and merged with her energy. We became one. I realized I was looking through her eyes and now looking out of the garage. I looked down at the rat, and he bowed to me with such reverence. He was beaming with pride. He had fulfilled his job of making the space for me to emerge. As I turned around to look at the box, it was gone along with the light. The light was in me. I became the light. I was holding the light. I was the light. I could hear her telling me "I am you. You are me. We are Tara."

I sat with this incredible transformation for a few minutes longer before I opened my eyes. I felt the strength of the two of us merged together into one. I felt my strength. As I opened my eyes, my therapist smiled at me. I'd been vocalizing this journey for her as I was experiencing it. She'd been with me second by second as it unfolded. I looked at her with different eyes. They didn't feel like the same eyes that had been looking at her ten minutes before. "Welcome," she said. I cried. I don't think she could have said anything more perfect to me than that.

I am in so much gratitude for Tara showing up in my life exactly as she did and when she did. It was perfect. I'm so grateful for the work I've done up to this point and continue to do to allow Tara to come into my life. It was as if I had to get to a certain point in my own journey of healing and awakening before she would reveal herself to me. And even then, it's taken me several years to let it all settle in and write about her and our experience.

A week after my profound meditation, I went to see my acupuncturist and relayed my experience to him. In some ways, this entire experience with the rat reminded me of how he has been helping me make way for this emergence. As soon as I tell him what's transpired in my life, he always knows what meridian is blocked or what body organ needs extra attention or if I'm ready to release shame that's been brought to the surface or if I need to integrate a profound experience like the one I'd just had. There was plenty to release and integrate given my recent revelation.

Whenever we release old stuff that's been hanging out inside, we make space for something new to emerge. By releasing these blocks from our body, we can step forward into a new opening, into more of who we are, into more love. As I was preparing to leave, he said, "In the Chinese zodiac, we're currently in the year of the rat!" This completely delighted me. Of course we were!

I knew there was more to come for me. But I was scared of what the other side looked like. I was scared to come out of my comfy, numb shell of denial. I was equally scared of staying the same. The call to move forward was stronger than remaining the same. Answering your own call takes bravery and discomfort. I chose myself. I chose to start having difficult conversations. I put myself first, even when I knew it was going to cause problems. I know you can relate to this. I know you've been in this position and have sometimes chosen to stay quiet to keep the peace. And it's okay. You always have a chance to choose again.

The choice to start on a journey of self-discovery can likely be one of the scariest times in our lives. As we think of all the things that could unfold for us if we started on this journey, we might realize our life could look incredibly different. We might upset people around us, and that can be crippling. We might start getting what we want, and we might not be used to that. We might not be used to getting even half of what we want. And this can cause self-sabotage. Something in us might tell us we don't deserve happiness. Our old unhealed wounds might want to tell us we're unworthy. We might not think we're strong enough to be on this journey. Because we know at our core that once we start on this incredible journey, there's no turning back. We can always take a pause, but there's no unknowing what we will learn. There's no unknowing how it feels when we acknowledge the ways we've been selling ourselves out for others.

We know there will be intense amounts of pain, sadness, loss, confusion, anger, and doubt, just as there will be happiness, joy, freedom, peace, stillness, and more love than we ever thought possible. And seriously, the potentiality of feeling all that, all those emotions, and the possibility of achieving and having everything we've imagined and dreamed of our whole lives can be scary AF! Just the thought of starting this journey can cause anxiety. This is why so many of us don't even take the first step. Even though we know that comfort requires discomfort, it can still be crippling. Even though the thought of who we might be at the end of the journey (our truest bright, shiny selves) might be overwhelming, we just know we can no longer stay in the sameness we've been in.

REMEMBERING

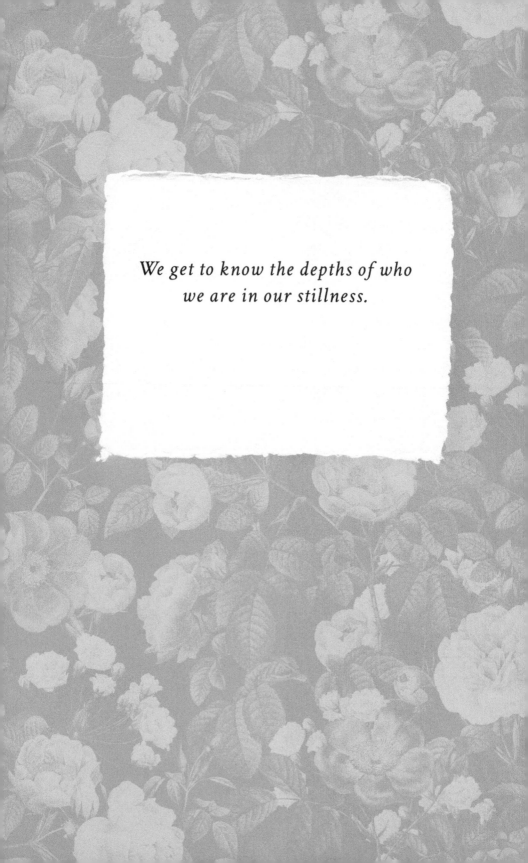

We get to know the depths of who
we are in our stillness.

3

SURRENDERING

In the spring of 2018, I walked away from my job. I'd been having this relentless gut feeling that something big was ready to reveal itself to me. And that if I kept working, I wouldn't have the space to hear and process what was ready to come out. More accurately, if I kept working, I wouldn't *make* the space to hear what was ready to come out. I'd just keep working, and my mind would be focused on work. And I loved what I was doing. But that intuitive voice was getting louder and louder.

Whenever I would sit down at my desk to work, I'd hear the same word, STOP! This internal push to walk away was big. And I was ignoring it. Honestly, I was confused and doubted what I was hearing. I was fully in denial that I was even interpreting this internal nudge properly. I'd be cooking dinner, going for a run, working out at the gym, or driving, and I'd hear it again: STOP! And just to make sure I wasn't misunderstanding, I finally asked this voice, "Stop what?" I heard, "Everything!" I listened and let that soak in for a while. *Stop everything? As in my business?* And again, I heard, "Stop everything." I was seriously confused. I felt like I was in alignment with what I was here to do.

I was in the middle of running my own business. I was coaching clients, hosted a weekly podcast, completed a website (re-)design, and had just returned from a writing retreat workshop excited and primed to start writing my book. I had just finished participating in a year-long coaching program that showed me how to get more clients, how to market myself better, and how to advertise. I'd also just finished hosting a very successful retreat in the mountains, which I love doing. It fuels me so much to hold space and guide women into themselves to uncover what they came to uncover and show them how to heal what they came to heal. In short, I was really invested on multiple levels in making what I had going work. It was fueling my soul. I could see the tangible results in those I was helping. I was more than confused. I felt duped. I felt like I was following the path of my soul only to be told to STOP? *Why is the Universe telling me this? I feel so aligned with my purpose.*

What was masquerading as skepticism was actually my own fear and denial. Fear and denial that there was something even bigger I was here to do. Fear that I was supposed to actually grab the microphone and get on stage, not just pretend anymore. At the same time, I knew I was here to be doing more than I currently was. I was also intuitively hearing not to start anything else, that there were things ready to be heard and healed. "That's your job right now," I was told. My ego didn't want to hear it. If I stopped working, then who was I? I started having conversations with myself. "If I stop everything, then what am I going to do? Just sit around?" And my Higher Self responded back with, "Take a break. Go to the pool. Read a book. Go outside. Take a hike. Do things you love to do and don't make time for. You need space to hear. You need space to heal."

At some point, it all started to sink in. I knew this was what I was supposed to do. It was the next step on my life journey. We all have a journey we're walking every day. Our lives unfold in phases. We quit a job. We begin a new job. We have kids. We move. We get married. We get divorced. This pause was my next phase, and I could feel its importance. I could feel layers ready to be shed, but I didn't know what those layers were. It just felt really important that I stop everything I was doing and make space to listen and trust the process.

But I was still afraid. I was afraid to tell my husband that I was getting the intuitive hit to stop my job and take a break. We'd spent so much time and money over the last many years that I was afraid he was going to be mad. It sounded wishy-washy to tell him that I was just going to stop. I didn't really blame him if he got mad. It's worth mentioning that, at the time, I was spending more money than I was making through taking courses, traveling to the courses, website development, and tech support. Starting your own business takes a lot of commitment. And I was committed to this on all levels. Truthfully though, our bank account could have used the break.

Finally, I mustered up the courage to tell him I kept getting the strong pull to stop all my business work to take a break and listen to myself. I told him I sensed I was ready for another layer of internal healing I currently didn't have time for. I told him I had no idea how long this would last and didn't know when or if I would start everything up again. And I didn't know what was ready to be uncovered. I only knew it was time to take a break.

To my relief and confusion, he was completely supportive. I didn't quite know what to think. The conversation was way too easy, and he was way too encouraging. He had always supported me in my endeavors. He never said, "We can't afford another course" or "Website development is how much?" like I was always waiting for. In that moment, he was offering me much more compassion and empathy than I was expecting. That highlighted my own confusion and curiosity in myself. In the recesses of my mind, I was wondering if this taking a break thing was just one more piece of me trying to figure out who I was. Was it one more thing I felt inspired to try that may or may not produce results? In my quest to find out who I am in this lifetime, I feel like I've tried it all. But this quitting still felt like a wild idea that I needed convincing of. I realized I needed to get away and think about all this. I needed to remove myself from our apartment and our everyday lives and be by myself so I could truly listen.

I made a reservation at the same retreat center my sisters and I had been to fifteen years before. Only this time, I wanted it to be a silent retreat for me. I knew I needed to get really quiet and listen to the guidance I was getting. I went for a long weekend. I woke up each morning at 5 a.m. to do ceremonies. I did yoga to open my body. I ate nourishing food the cooks had chanted over. They served us freshly made granola, warm soups made with ingredients from their garden, and delicious fruit pies made from scratch. I hiked in the mountains and breathed in the fresh, invigorating smell of pine trees. I sat and took in the landscape that was in front of me: gorgeous mountains full of pine trees, meadows with blooming wildflowers, and a pond off in the distance. I meditated daily.

Being purposefully silent for four days is bliss. My mind slowed down. I wasn't prepping a response for someone, thinking of what to say next, or worried about saying hi. My mind was spacious and open with so much quietness. The same thing kept coming to me over and over: it was time to stop all the work I was doing because big things were ready to be healed.

One thing I learned from being silent for four days is that way too many thoughts spun in my head when I was working. No wonder I was getting the push to stop. There was too much noise. And the noise was keeping me from hearing what was ready to come up and be healed.

When we are full of internal wounding, we'll seek a constant amount of external noise to keep all this wounding at bay. We need the news, music, conversation, audiobooks, podcasts, people, activities, TV in the background, and so on to keep our minds occupied. I'm not saying all of this is bad. What I'm inviting is an honest look at how much of this external noise is going on because, ultimately, if we have a lot, we might be in denial of our deepest feelings. When the mind is not occupied, our old wounds have the potential to surface and we might see or feel them. And if we see them or feel them, then we might feel the need to take action. And if we feel the need to take action, we might be opening a can of worms we're not ready for or don't feel we have the resources to support us. Maybe we're afraid of what others will think if we stop and slow down. The healing changes we decide to make might affect those around us. So, for some of us, it's easier to keep our minds occupied with all this external noise so the pain doesn't bubble up. It's also exhausting. When we're in this way of life, we don't usually recognize it. It's all we know.

Keeping our attention outside ourselves in busyness can keep us numb to our own pain, giving us a false sense of security and safety. We get to pretend that all is well. The opportunity to do any type of healing won't even present itself when we stay this engaged with external noise.

Quiet space is what gives us the capacity to allow thoughts and memories to flow in. The soft quiet space we create allows us to listen. This is what this retreat and therapy offered me. This is where I began to know myself. We get to know the depths of who we are in our stillness. We begin to find the wounded parts of us that are ready to be healed. We find a safe place so we can dive in and find the dark crevices. And as we heal these dark places, the stillness provides us a place of strength and knowingness of who we are.

In my meditations, I kept getting the intuitive hit that past wounds, past actions, things left unsaid were ready to see the light of day. It was as if all this was just under the surface and all I had to do was show up and be present. Truly, my job was just to be me. Ironically, isn't that what we're all here to do anyway ... just be ourselves? I could feel the percolation. I was nervous. I wondered what was ready to come to the surface.

While I'd seen different therapists pretty consistently for the previous fifteen years, I didn't have one as this deeper call came in. I wondered if I should find one to help me through this, but when I tuned in and asked myself this question, I got a big NO. I heard my intuition telling me that I could do this one just fine on my own and that I had lots of healers around me that would also help me in this uncovering. And that which was ready to come up was going to come up anyway. I returned home from that weekend completely confident that I needed to stop working and make space for this to occur.

At the same time this was unfolding, my husband, George, was in the middle of a year-long intensive personal coaching program, which put him in a completely different mind space than I'd seen him in before. He was purposefully bringing up his old wounds and triggers to heal them. He was letting go of so much of his old baggage that my Higher Self knew I'd be safe in uncovering whatever I was ready to uncover. When I knew he was behind me, it was as if the Universe was standing next to me, showing me how my life could move and shift to make space for this next piece. And, I heard my intuition again talking to me, asking me what other excuse I was going to use not to take this break. I couldn't come up with any.

That following week, I stopped all the things I had in motion. I shut off my website, sent notes to my coaching clients, letting them know I was going to take a break, and put away all the material I'd brought back from the writing retreat months prior. I sent out notes to people whom I'd been creating new content with. I cleaned off my desk.

I was really sad. I could feel the ending happening. It was a big deal for me to stop everything. I was so committed to my work. I loved what I was doing. I felt like I was letting so many people down. I felt like I was letting my business down. In some ways, I felt like I was failing. Failing my husband, failing my clients, failing myself, failing my purpose for being here. But there was also a teeny part of me that was thrilled to not have any formal responsibility other than my family. It kind of felt like a stay-cay. But even in that, I felt guilty. I was conflicted, sad, kind of excited, and kind of scared.

The rest of the week, I was a bit lost. I didn't really know what to do with myself. It was similar to the feeling I had when my last kid went to school. I had the entire day to myself and just stood in the living room with no idea what to do. So many things ran through my mind that I *could* do, but I felt paralyzed and lost. This was so incredibly similar. Was I having another identity crisis?

It felt weird. I was in my late forties and I wasn't working. I felt slightly useless. My husband encouraged me to go to the pool, and I remember thinking, *Who goes to the pool in the middle of the day in the middle of the week? And what if someone sees me? What are they going to think? Will they think I don't have a job, which means I don't do anything? Will they think I'm some middle-aged woman who lives off of her husband?* I was afraid of the (inner) voices telling me I wasn't important or that I wasn't contributing to society. I didn't want anyone to judge me like I'd obviously done to so many other women. For me to move forward with this journey, I had to admit these truths to myself.

Our judgments are our own unhealed wounds showing themselves to us. Often, we judge others because there's deep underlying pain within us that we don't want anyone to see. Our psyche tells us we should feel ashamed of certain experiences we've had, so we subconsciously put up some pretty solid walls so no one else will see this shame. Our ego thinks all is well. When, really, we're just perpetuating our own pain. Our judgments toward others hurt everyone, including ourselves. Why couldn't I just be with the thought that these women had a day off and were enjoying themselves? Why was I assuming they were doing anything other than enjoying themselves? Better yet, why did I think any of it was my business in the first place?

With all these thoughts rolling around my head, I went to

the pool anyway. And I took a book, a fiction book, another crazy thing for me to do—read fiction. For years I'd read almost every self-help and motivational book I could get my hands on. But at this moment, I was getting the intuitive hit of not to read self-help books, that I didn't need any help with what I was going to experience and that someone else's perspective would interfere with my own. Gasp! I had a fiction book, at the pool, in the middle of the day, in the middle of the week.

The other people at the pool seemed to be relaxed and happy, whereas I was a nervous wreck. I was completely out of my comfort zone. What if someone asked me why I was there? I thought if I could just look like I knew what I was doing, like I deserved this time, maybe I would put off that convincing vibe and no one would bother me. Of course, someone bothered me!

Out of all the available lounge chairs at the pool, a woman put her towel on the chair right next to me. She asked me what I did. (I know this was the Universe at work.) My brain got so busy at that moment with how I wanted to respond. I wanted to give her my verbal resume and tell her everything I'd done over the last five years. Actually, I wanted to tell her everything I'd done over the last 20 years so she would think I really deserved this break I was taking. I'd been raising three boys, mostly on my own, following my military husband all over the world. I was also active in the military community, serving on boards, working when I could, starting several businesses, constantly volunteering in my kids' schools. I could go on. I'd been busy from morning till night, just like I was taught. This mental chatter made it clear that I still didn't think I deserved a break. I wanted this woman to think highly of me and not judge me, and I wanted to tell her some version of what just unloaded in my mind. But, instead, my Higher Self jumped in immediately and answered for me: "I'm taking a break right now." And that was that.

It was hard for me to just *be* with taking a break. It was hard for me to be okay with not working. It made me nervous. I knew the anxiety I was feeling was something more than just stopping all my work. I realized my work had become my identity, just as it had for the women before me. That's who I was. It's what I would tell people so they would think I was important. My work was what gave me the feeling I was contributing to society, that I was making a difference and that I was somehow following this elusive path of helping the world. If I was taking time off, who was I? Was I still an important part of the family? To what was I supposed to attach my sense of self-worth? I felt ashamed for taking a break from work to have time for myself. It went against everything I'd been taught and seen my whole life.

Here's what I knew the female to look like growing up: she wanted to be strong and independent while simultaneously submissive to her husband. Her husband had the last word and made the decisions. Even though the man was the provider, the woman worked hard all day long, harder than anyone in the family. There was never any time to rest or take a break, let alone stop everything they were doing like I was. I know these women in my family were taught that their self-worth came from how hard they could work all day long. If you kept busy working, you were worthy and had importance. It meant you were alive. You were somebody. You had value. So when I began to dissect my beliefs about what a powerful woman was and who I wanted to become, I didn't have anyone immediate to look to.

We all have this busyness going on to a certain extent. Unless we've consciously chosen to slow down, our lives are pretty full. Everyone around us is busy. We judge people by how busy they are or aren't. When they're busy, we think they must be an upstanding citizen. Surely they're contributing to society if they're so busy. And if we judge someone to not be busy, we usually think they're lazy or have nothing better to do. I was thoroughly confused as to what the female was supposed to be. Was this way of being, the constant business and external noise that I shared with the women before me, also their way of avoiding pain and feeling? Were they trying to avoid their own deeper wounds or inner self-doubts? Did they want more out of life but knew it was best to just keep it to themselves?

I was also struggling with my inner knowing that I had a bigger mission on this planet to fulfill. Somewhere in the depths of my soul, I knew I was here for way more than what I was currently doing. So, if I wasn't working toward that goal, what the hell was I doing? I wasn't feeling important. I wasn't feeling seen. I was utterly lost!

As I look back now, this was the start of the healing. I was learning how to surrender to a process directed from deep within without knowing what the end result would be. I was learning how to trust like I'd never trusted before. I was learning how to listen and respond to my intuition. And, I was learning about the judgments I held toward other women, which were really a reflection of the judgments I had of myself and where I found my worth. These woundings we hold onto run deep within our psyche.

It took weeks of me unwinding and letting go before things began to surface. When you have a train moving at a fast speed, it takes that train a long time to slow down. When we have beliefs set up of what our life is supposed to look like, what a woman looks like, what we're supposed to be doing in the world, it takes a while to see, much less deconstruct, those beliefs. We think our beliefs are absolute. That's why we believe them. And normally, we don't second guess what we believe until we experience something that jars us and we question what we've believed to be true.

I fought against my beliefs about taking time off and what I should be doing instead. There was so much guilt wrapped up in letting go. Eventually, I started wondering what it would look like if I pretended to enjoy my time off. I wasn't yet allowing myself to have fun, and pretending sounded way easier. Leaning into fully enjoying myself felt too raw. So I pretended. I pretended I was enjoying myself at the pool, all the while still wondering what others were thinking of me.

In those weeks and months of unwinding, I started to notice a softness and stillness slowly coming over me. I was slowing down. I was giving myself space. Was I finding a balance? I was learning how to enjoy myself, not just pretend. There was quiet space in my brain. Even though I was full of doubt and metaphorically kicking, screaming, and squirming in my seat, I was surrendering in the only way I knew how. I was following my intuition, taking it day by day, and seeing what unfolded as I continued to trust.

Amidst all my outdoor time, I realized I had been teaching and coaching for years on how to trust the process, how to surrender to the Universe. You know that old saying, "We teach what we need to learn?" I'd been teaching others how to surrender and trust, even in a process that has no guaranteed outcome. I needed to trust and surrender differently than I'd done before.

When I refer to this process as surrendering, I don't mean lying down and giving up, thinking everything is going to work itself out and be peachy. Surrendering just means that you're surrendering to the outcome and trusting that your higher power and your soul know what's best for you.

Starting this process of surrendering and trusting can feel clunky. Maybe you've never done this before, trusting in something other than yourself. And maybe you don't even trust yourself. Ever thought about whether or not you actually trust yourself? I didn't. But I came to find there was a degree to which I didn't actually trust myself. It never occurred to me that an inner part of me really knew what was best for me or that this journey was for my greater good. None of this crossed my mind. I was learning as I was going. Trusting and surrendering did NOT come naturally to me.

When we're in fear and we don't trust, our nervous system is always in a fight or flight mode. Most likely, our adrenals are burnt out. When our adrenals are burnt out, it causes all kinds of physical and emotional effects. We don't think we can trust our body because it's always sick or acting up. We think it's failing us. Fear doesn't foster trust and surrender. By the time I started seeing a naturopathic doctor, I learned I had adrenal fatigue, among many other things happening in my body. I didn't know how to trust. I didn't know what I needed to take care of me. I didn't know how to speak up for myself or even that I had a right to speak up for myself. I had no idea that my needs, whatever they were, were actually important. What I realize now is that I was embarking on a complete overhaul of my life, not only in trust and surrender but in shifting everything.

When we put the two together—surrender and trust—it means that we ask for what we want and then let it go and trust that everything that comes to us is in our highest and best interests. And that's the hard part, the trusting. It's not always easy to let go. It's hard to not want to manipulate the outcome or try to influence it in some way. As humans, we want to know what's going to happen. I chuckle at myself sometimes because I'll give my issues or concerns to the Universe and then wonder what's going to happen. I'll try to guess when I'll get an answer or how it's going to come to me or what the end result will be.

Surrendering means we know everything will always work out perfectly, given what we came here to experience. Trusting means we realize everything is unfolding perfectly, even when it's incredibly hard. Everything we do in life supports what we came here to learn and teach. It's our job to listen and find out what those pieces are. We are always dancing in tandem with the Universe at any given moment. We are always perfectly on point. It can be no other way! The Divine always has a bigger plan for us. WE have a bigger plan for us. And it's usually something greater than we can ever imagine.

SURRENDERING

*Everything that happens to us
happens for us. It's all happening
perfectly.*

4

TRUSTING

I was indoctrinated into religion the minute I was born. I was taught there was a higher power outside of me and his name was God. From the very beginning, I learned about God the Father, God the Son, and God the Holy Spirit, the trifecta of male patriarchy. I was taught the very tip-top of the church, the Pope, was a man. I was baptized and had my first communion, first confession, and confirmation, all at the hands of men. I was married in the church by a man. I was given all the gateways to life, according to my religion, by a man. In addition, I was supposed to fear this man who was teaching me. I was supposed to fear the man up in the clouds or standing at the pulpit. He was laying down judgment on me according to what I did or didn't do.

If I wasn't a "good girl," then I would probably go to Hell. And if I was a good girl, then I might go to Heaven, but those good-girl boundaries were loose. I was never quite sure if it was a literal meaning or a soft suggestion. Going through

Catholic grade school and high school, we had religion classes every day. We went to church at least once during the school week. We were constantly taught about the wrath of God. In grade school, when it was our turn to go to confession, I had to tattle on myself. I thought it was crazy that I had to go to confession so some man could give me prayers I had to say to beg for forgiveness and ensure I would remain in the good graces of God so I could go to Heaven. Usually, I would tell the priest that I stuck my tongue out at someone I didn't like or that I had said bad words to another girl or had bad thoughts about a teacher. Was I going to Hell?

There didn't seem to be any room for mistakes. There was confession and paying for my sins. The church taught me that I was supposed to trust and surrender to this man in the sky. I couldn't. I didn't trust him. There was nothing safe about it for me. This God of my upbringing seemed judgy and righteous, and the thought of trusting that higher power was scary, frightening, and made me feel small. Fear doesn't foster trust and surrender. It fosters control, judgment of others, competitiveness, feelings of being less than, and more fear. Growing up, I thought this line of fear was how life worked. I thought I was supposed to be afraid of all the adults around me and especially God. I was afraid to question or second guess what they said.

Everything that I was told—that God was this all-knowing, judging man who sat up in the clouds watching me, waiting for me to mess up—was contradictory to what I secretly felt about him. I felt like this energy was really loving, accepting, fun, and not at all like the divisive, shaming, judging man the church wanted me to believe in. But I was a kid, and I was doing and thinking what I was told. I was still young enough to believe that the adults around me knew what was best for me and thought they would never lead me astray. So, I put my own thoughts aside and believed what I was told. I really thought that even though I had my own ideas, everyone else knew what was best. While I could hear that little voice telling me there was another way, she got me in trouble, so I kept her silent.

Trusting in that fearful version of a higher power taught me I didn't know what was best for me. I wasn't taught to ask myself what I thought was best for me. Actually, let me correct that. When I'd done something wrong, I was told to ask myself what I thought. And I was told I should be feeling ashamed of myself for doing whatever it was I did, not checking in to see how I actually felt. Nothing about that felt good. It taught me that if I went internally to check out how I felt, I'd better be feeling ashamed rather than getting curious about how I felt. Feeling shame feels terrible. No one wants to feel that.

Yet, in my religion, this is how I was raised. The one act of going to confession to a man and having to be forgiven by a man set up so many other patterns in my life. Subconsciously, I was always looking to a man to grant me acceptance and approval, to tell me I was good enough, that I wasn't bad. I looked to men to tell me what was right and wrong. It taught me men were in charge and would always have the last word.

It taught me to look to a man for recognition. I was constantly looking for male approval to validate my sheer existence on the planet. This need for acceptance and approval was quietly setting up my need for external validation. I was subconsciously on the hunt for a man who would ultimately tell me what to do, what to say, and how to behave and to validate me as a woman. I didn't know how to look within and figure out how I felt or what I needed.

Many years later, starting with my first therapist, I began questioning the teachings of the church. They weren't resonating with me anymore. As I was deconstructing my religious beliefs, I realized what I'd been taught: that my supposedly divine relationship with the man who created me was a one-sided relationship. I felt I had no say in our relationship, I was afraid of him, and he was the final judge and jury of my behavior. Growing up, I was told that when I talked to God, I shouldn't ask for too much. I should pray for everyone else and for my own flawed soul, and not question what God said. Even as an adult, I still believed God was an old man with a beard. A man that I couldn't really talk to or talk back to. I couldn't really have a conversation that I wanted to have with him. I didn't have a voice with this male figure.

The way I was brought up to think about God didn't support me as a female using my voice and being out in the world either. According to the Bible and my religion, women weren't as powerful as men. Outshining a man was just not done. Speaking my truth might be seen as a competition with a man. The God I was brought up with was judging me and was subliminally telling me that men were in charge. I never got the feeling that men and women were equal in the world. What I learned showed me men were a step above women. Wounded parts of me that I had yet to uncover told me I was put here on this planet to serve men however they saw fit. It felt like brainwashing. It was teaching me that women were here to serve men.

This left incredible gaps in my own sense of grounding. Who was I supposed to be? Was I really here to only be of service to men? Was there nothing else to look forward to? When I would think about these questions, which wasn't very often because it was scary, I felt doomed, deflated, and destined to live a life that wasn't mine. I couldn't conceive that this God of my upbringing would support my thoughts of being bright and shiny out in the world or doing healing work in the world. I had no examples of that. My current understanding of a man wouldn't allow me to be big in the world. And if, in fact, the life I was to lead was being determined by a man, then I might never fulfill my purpose. Yet, there was still a sliver of light that kept telling me I was here for something different. In the depths of my being, I still knew I was here for a greater purpose. It was my intuition speaking to me. The intuition that I was never taught to listen to. I clung to that.

One by one, I began dissecting the beliefs I'd been taught. I realized I no longer believed the patriarchal agenda my religion wanted me to believe in. Eventually, I left. Actually, my family left. My husband and I talked about it and decided we could have our own relationship with God and we could teach our boys to discover their own relationship with a higher power. We didn't need a middleman, our priest, to tell us what was expected of us.

After I finally left the church, I started exploring the relationship I wanted to have with this creator. I realized the conversations I was beginning to have were completely different from the ones I was told I could have. When we decide we're ready to talk to our higher power, it can look however we want it to look. We can speak out loud, we can do it silently, we can journal it, we can sing it, we can shout it. Whatever feels perfect for you is perfect for the Universe.

When I started shifting my thoughts away from the God I'd been raised with to a new higher power, I got to decide what I wanted to call it. Some people call it Goddess, Spirit, God, All That Is, Creator, Universe, Buddha, Allah, or simply refer to it as energy. Mine is interchangeable depending on my mood. Although, at times, referring to this energy as God still triggers me. When I get triggered by it, I just acknowledge that I'm triggered and choose another word. Ultimately, we're all talking about the same higher power. So, the name is what fits you personally.

When I began my own relationship with this higher power, I also started exploring other religions and cultures. I realized other religions had amazing relationships with their creator. Their creator was loving, kind, helpful, and accepting. Other belief systems taught love instead of fear and acceptance rather than judgment, rejection, and division. Exploring so many different religions and cultures allowed me to decide for myself what I wanted my relationship with a higher power to be. I knew I wanted it to be loving and warm and non-judgmental. I wanted to know that my voice was being heard. I wanted to know that no matter how many wrong things I had done in my life, this energy, this higher power, was still going to love me.

The more I grew in my own faith in a different higher power, the more I felt loved and accepted by it. I was learning that this higher power was an energy of love and acceptance, an energy that didn't see right or wrong, only experiences and choices that move us to the next experience and choice. And the more I felt accepted, the more those feelings flowed to those around me. I found it easier to love and accept others and to see their choices as experiences they were having rather than judging them and seeing their choices as divisive.

The teachings I'd grown up with, that judgment and separation were all around, began falling away and were replaced with love, acceptance, and curiosity. It was way easier to learn to surrender to this higher power that was so benevolent than it had been to even think about surrendering to the previous higher power I'd been brought up with. I would have been surrendering myself to a male energy that may or may not condemn me at any given moment. I couldn't do it. I couldn't be vulnerable with that God. I didn't feel loved or supported by the first one.

The God of my choosing wasn't going to strike me down or judge my deepest thoughts or desires, no matter how bad they seemed. I trusted that whenever I brought a problem to my meditation or just talked to this energy, I would receive an answer. I knew that trusting and surrendering to this creator was exactly what I'd been looking for.

Trusting and surrendering can be a little bit easier once we realize that we, ourselves, our soul, actually set up our life before we came here and that every single experience we have is no mistake. We're never doing the wrong thing. Everything is learning and gathering information for our next experience. There is no right or wrong. It just is. I know that can be a big one to wrap our heads around—that we planned everything before we came here—but we did. Before we incarnated, we chose the lessons we wanted to learn, we chose our parents for what we would learn, we chose the major life experiences according to what we came here to learn. We also chose all these experiences according to what we're here to do.

When we can surrender to a higher power that fits for us, we can receive the information and knowingness of why we're here. I get the feeling the previous God I believed in never would have let me get as big in the world as I know I'm supposed to be. That God taught me that I was supposed to be humble. Being a woman and a powerhouse on the planet, delivering a message to the masses doesn't feel like it would be in alignment with my old version of God. Ushering in the Divine Feminine doesn't feel like the same agenda the old

God had for me. I couldn't do what I'm here to do if I still subscribed to those old beliefs.

I've longed to know why I'm here for as long as I can remember. I've been asking God and everyone else around me if they knew why I was here. Just like so many other things in my life, I was looking externally for this answer and validation. I didn't know how to go inward to my own sense of knowing. Now that I have a different relationship with this higher power, I feel safe going within and trusting the intuition and information I get. I deeply desire to know the enormity and purpose of my being here on this planet. And for me to know that, I have to continually ask for help from a higher power and trust the guidance I'm given every day, even when the guidance doesn't seem to make sense or when the outcome isn't immediately available.

I've learned that the Universe works behind the scenes on our behalf quite often. Things have to be shifted around for us, and it's up to us to be patient. This is trust. When we've asked for a major shift, often it takes a while for an answer or a resolution to come to us. The Universe might show us the steps on how to make the changes we want. For example, if we know we're not happy in our current life and the Universe gives us lots of messages to quit our jobs, it's up to us to take that information and move forward. We've given the Universe the information that we're not happy; the Universe has given us the guidance to quit our jobs. That's when we get to trust and know that it's all perfect. Even if we don't have another job lined up, maybe we can just do it anyway and trust the forward movement of what wants to unfold.

When we get this kind of information without anything else, it can be easy to get down on ourselves and think we're doing this surrendering thing all wrong or that we don't know how to listen or that our guides aren't talking to us. What the Universe is really offering to us in this moment is the opportunity to become extremely good at listening and surrendering. The Universe is always taking care of us, even when it looks otherwise.

When we're in the middle of some crazy, traumatic stuff, it can seem like the Universe has forgotten about us or that we're just too flawed for the Universe to love us. When we're in the depths of depression or grief and can't find our way out, it can seem like the higher power we believe in is nowhere to be found. But if we believe that we've chosen everything we will experience here on the planet, it can give us a bit of comfort knowing there is a higher reason for everything. Everything that happens to us happens for us. It's all happening perfectly. That thought alone can give us strength and trust that we are always in the perfect place at the perfect time, doing exactly what we're supposed to be doing. Always! Otherwise, we'd be somewhere else.

Surrendering and trusting go hand in hand. You can't have one without the other. Once we've surrendered to our higher power, then we get to trust that everything that comes to us is perfect. And I know that sounds crazy sometimes. I've coached people who have a hard time believing this—that their own crazy or addictive behavior is perfect—but it is. Or that their partner's crazy or addictive behavior is perfect. It is. It's perfect for the lessons we came here to learn about ourselves. It's perfect for everyone around us who came here to learn lessons from us. It's the ripple effect again. We're all here, on this planet, helping each other come back to ourselves. It's why I said in the intro to this book that everyone in my life has been a teacher by being exactly who they are. If they had not been perfectly who they are on their own journey, I would not have had the opportunity to grow in the way I did and still do.

If we can look at our experiences from the perspective that everything we do is perfect and we are all learning as we go, it takes us out of a victim place and puts us in a place of knowing that our life is right on track. We can begin to trust our own journey. And when we get curious about our journey and get curious about what we're here to learn and what we're here to do, we can really surrender. It's the moment our life will begin to flow.

The trusting and surrendering I was leaning into after I stopped working was different from what I'd done before. I was going deeper. I had to trust that the path I was on was exactly perfect for me. It became my daily practice to remind myself that everything I was experiencing was perfect, that I was perfect, and that this unfolding I was leaning into was leading me to the perfect place. When we know we are doing exactly what we are supposed to be doing and trusting that all is perfect, we can relax into the knowingness that the Universe is here to guide us and take care of us.

Maybe you started life trusting in a higher power but have had experiences that led you to doubt that a higher power is taking care of you. Maybe you've felt egregiously let down or have had a serious tragedy in your life, which led you to believe there isn't a God. Wherever you are on this journey, if you choose, you can shift this part of you that doesn't trust. Maybe you're here to learn to trust yourself. Maybe you're here to learn to trust in a higher power. Maybe it's to learn how to trust and surrender. If it's any of these things, you can do it. Ultimately trusting in ourselves and trusting in a higher power is one and the same. We are the higher power. We are our own God source. We have direct connection to and are part of the collective. We're a part of the whole.

Since we are part of all that is, the higher power, we're surrendering to the overall plan that WE created for ourselves before we incarnated here—WE, us and the Universe. And I put *we* in capital letters because WE are part of the higher power. It is in us. We are the God power within ourselves. It just takes retraining our brains and working with our nervous systems to learn to trust again.

When we trust and surrender to a higher power, we are letting go and surrendering to us and to the Universe. Nothing will ever go wrong. WE will always have our best interests at heart. We might think things are going wrong, but really, it's only an experience. There is no right or wrong. We have experiences that lead us to our next moment, and by means of the experiences we have, we will make choices on how we experience the next moment. Every choice we make in the moment leads us to our next moment. And so on.

Being able to trust that I am it and it is me and it is all happening simultaneously allows me to surrender to this journey. I know I'm not alone; I'm a part of it all. There are greater powers helping me every day. Surrendering to this knowing and trusting this process has now become my go-to method of doing life and has gotten me to this point on my journey. Even when I struggle with surrendering, I know I just have to trust.

Having a trusting relationship with ourselves as the Universe and knowing that we are loved and taken care of allows us to trust in the unfolding of ourselves. It allows us to be more present moment by moment every day. It gives us a safe place to be seen. We can let go of the incredibly tight hold we've had on our lives. We can allow the Universe to guide us, to show us the way, and we can trust in this guidance we're getting because we are the Universe. Life can be so much easier when we know there is a loving, present energy that, at every moment, has our best interests at heart. We can surrender into our lives, knowing we are supported by ourselves and by the greater good.

When you surrender to this knowing, it can be a process or may come completely natural to you. It might take you months or years to let go of all the old behaviors and beliefs you've had in your mind of what a God is and does. Don't judge yourself, and don't be hard on yourself. Let all this unfold naturally. Just observe it all. Ask the Universe to guide you through this process. Be aware and mindful of your thoughts and be active in this process. When we're reprogramming, it takes time and self-love.

It has taken me the greater part of twenty years to come to these new beliefs and let go of the old. And really, they're more than beliefs, they are my knowing. It's been through therapy, research, reading, observing, and listening to my own guidance that I've realized *I* get to make my life exactly as I want it to be, that *I'm* in charge of me, that *I am* the creator of what happens to me and for me every day. I've realized my life is happening for me, not to me. And that I am part of a greater plan of a whole creative process that is full of love.

TRUSTING

*When we release the darkness,
light floods in. Light is love. Love
is the Divine Feminine.*

5

CONNECTING

Growing up in my family, we never talked about sex. It was taboo. It came with a lot of unwritten rules. Religion gave me plenty of messages about sex. The Bible talks about Mary Magdalene and what a horrible outcast she was. Mother Mary had Jesus but didn't have sex, and the rest of the wives in the Bible were being submissive and doing their wifely duties by having sex. Kids in school gave me messages about sex; they would talk about the "sluts" who were having sex. My high school anatomy class taught me about sex from the perspective of telling me about the male and female bodies, their reproductive organs, and what the utilitarian purposes were. It was all super serious, and we didn't get to ask many questions.

In addition to being something saved for marriage, I was taught by the Bible that sex was only to procreate. And since no one else that I knew in an authoritarian role talked about it as fun and something to explore, I didn't think it was supposed to be fun or feel good. The Bible never referred to it in this way. Because these thoughts and feelings were on continual replay in my mind, I knew this was the next piece of my healing: my own relationship with sex.

It had only been a couple months since I'd stopped working. I'd had a couple realizations and breakthroughs, and they were good, but the breakthroughs were slowing down. I started wondering if that was it. Did I stop working for that? Growth really comes in waves for me. I get deep in the middle of growth, which includes feeling the trigger or seeing the old wound, then allowing myself to face it and feel it and see exactly how it's affected my life, then I flow out of it, implement what I've learned, and ride the wave for a while. And just when I think I'm comfortable, a new wave will come to pull me in, and I see another wound or trigger that's ready to be seen and healed. Another round of growing and releasing begins.

As I began wondering what was coming next to be seen and healed, questions about my own sexuality started popping into my head. I started thinking about my sex life with my husband. Sometimes when we'd have sex, I didn't really feel present, like I wasn't in my body. My body would be participating, but the sensations I thought I was supposed to be having weren't all there. My mind wandered. I'd wonder if we were done yet. Most of the time, he was way more excited than me. Why was this? Were my hormones imbalanced? Did guys just really enjoy sex more than girls? Why wasn't I as into it as he was? Sometimes I secretly thought it was a chore. Why? But here's what's strange.

Other times I couldn't get enough of it. I wanted more. It would be on my mind constantly. I was seriously confused about this rollercoaster of emotions I was on.

I contacted my friend and healer. Over the years, she and I had uncovered a lot of my unhealed and repressed trauma. I knew she was the exact person to help me get into this one. I knew there was more to it than I could find by myself. She uses tapping and other modalities to find out what the body is holding onto. Our body holds onto emotions and trauma if we don't know how to properly process and release them. This trauma, both physical and emotional, gets stuck in our cells, in our muscles, in our organs. And when we don't properly process the trauma and let it out, our body creates ways to let it out, like illness, disease, aches and pains, and "accidents." We adopt addictive patterns to avoid feeling too much. Our body becomes numb, and we don't have access to the full range of emotions available to us. The truth is, most of us don't know all this is going on in our bodies. We've been duped into thinking our bodies aren't this smart. We haven't been taught how to properly listen to all the signs our body gives us daily. The fact is, our bodies are incredibly smart. It's part of the makeup of our genes. It's really good at telling us what's going on.

When the day came to have my Zoom call, I found myself nervous and anxious. I wanted to cancel our session. I wanted to find some reason why this wasn't a good idea. I knew this was my ego's way of not wanting to uncover whatever was there, and whatever was there was probably pretty big. My ego was trying to do some serious backtracking to get out of this, which confirmed even more to me that I was on the right track. This session was a must. Another piece of my puzzle was ready to reveal itself to me.

As we dove into the session, a repressed memory of sexual abuse surfaced. With my eyes closed, I tapped through some emotions and returned to a moment when I was very young. The memory came flooding back of a man putting his penis in my mouth and ejaculating. I couldn't breathe. I felt stifled, gagged. During the moment of the abuse, everything around me stopped. The essence of me stopped. I left my body. All of a sudden, I was watching it happen from a vantage point up above. I felt nothing. I saw this all unfolding, but I wasn't in my body.

As I recalled that first experience of sexual abuse and watched myself leave my body, I believe my soul was fractured. I believe the trauma was too much for my small body and mind to comprehend.

When we experience any kind of abuse or trauma, our souls can fracture as a way to manage what's happening. A piece of us leaves. And I wondered, since mine fractured while in an act of sex, was this the reason I was constantly trying to have sex in high school? Not only to feel love but also to get my body back? Maybe my unconscious mind thought the only way back into my body was through sex. Maybe I thought sex was the portal, so I had as much of it as I could, trying to reclaim myself.

After he finished, he threatened me and told me, if I spoke to anyone about it, I would be punished. This was the first experience I can remember where I was told not to talk and knew it wasn't safe if I spoke up. He was telling me to lie, to not speak my truth. And if I did speak my truth, somehow he would punish me. He was telling me to protect him instead of me. He made himself more important than me. He put his needs over mine. He was essentially telling me, even though he had just abused me and taken advantage of me, that if I spoke up for myself and told my truth against him, a man, I would be punished.

Much like what I learned from the church, I believed it wasn't safe to speak up for myself. I believed speaking up would get me in serious trouble. I believed telling the truth would bring me punishment. Since he told me I would be punished, my very young mind internalized this to mean *I* was wrong and *I* was bad, and since he said I would be punished, somehow it must be my fault. Lifelong patterns of taking the blame and believing I would always be in trouble for telling the truth started at that exact moment.

My lifelong perception of men and my relationship with them started here (and was reinforced even more by what I was taught in the church). I lied for men because that's what was expected. On an incredibly twisted level, when I lied for a man to keep them out of trouble, I was waiting for them to tell me I'd done it right, that the lying and sacrificing myself was exactly what I was supposed to be doing. I was waiting for them to tell me, "Good job, you got it right." I know now that at the exact moment of the abuse, I formed many unconscious beliefs about how I operated in the world.

It left me with an unconscious program running in my psyche: I would default to male demands. I would put their needs and happiness over mine. When it came to men, I believed I didn't have a choice in life. Saying no meant potentially getting in trouble with a man or not being liked by a man. If they told me to do something, it was in my best interest to just do it. This later showed up as settling. Since I believed I didn't have a choice, I would settle for whatever was happening, even when it wasn't what I wanted. I believed my body and my mind no longer belonged to me.

When my session ended that day in tears, I felt sad, mad, ashamed, betrayed, shocked, and in disbelief. Shocked because as I sat, letting this all settle, I'd vaguely remembered writing this memory down in a journal years and years before. At the time I wrote it down, I didn't believe myself. I thought something in me was making this up. I didn't feel connected to the memory. Now I realized I wasn't making it up. I found my earlier journal and read almost the exact same recollection that I'd just uncovered in my session. With all the emotions I was feeling, I also felt relief. I was relieved that this piece of remembering was out of me. I'd brought it out of the darkness and into the open and let it see the light of day. It no longer held the power over me that it had for decades. Now I could begin this piece of my healing.

As I moved forward with this information, I thought surely this was all there was. What I didn't realize at the time was that all the sexual experiences I've ever had were tainted by this initial one. The memories of subsequent sexual experiences, good and bad, were still hanging out way in the back of my mind. For years after that session, these memories would randomly make their way into my awareness and I would shut them down. Kind of like when you put old belongings you're not sure what to do with in a box and store them in the basement so you can deal with them later. And later comes, and you look at them and still don't want to deal with them, so you close the box and leave it where you initially put it. You tell yourself that one day you'll get to all the old stuff, just not right now. That's what I'd done with my sexual memories. I put them in a box, and I thought I closed the lid. Tight. But every now and then they came back. I'd look at them, be slightly curious as to why they would pop up, and then close the box again. I kind of wondered why they kept doing this. Some of these memories weren't great. Actually, most of them weren't great. So why did they keep showing up? But that's as far as I went with the curiosity. Until now.

One thing I've learned is that healing isn't linear. It doesn't happen all at once. It's been four years since that session, and it's taken me this long to realize there was so much more to be healed. It's time to open up the box that's been stored away all these years and figure out why these memories have been showing themselves to me throughout the years.

When I began unpacking these memories, something was missing. I wasn't going deep enough. I couldn't find what I was looking for. There was more to be uncovered, and I wasn't getting it. As I continued to dig deeper, I started to remember a lot of the sexual experiences I've had and how they affected me. I allowed the details of these experiences to come forward, and they started to feel heavy.

As I was processing and writing about these experiences, I was having a hard time with the shame I was feeling about what I'd done and what had happened to me. I felt ashamed that some of the experiences were fun and I liked them, and others I didn't like. The latter made me feel numb and ashamed. I didn't speak up for myself and say no. Even though it's been more than two decades since I left the church, the shame from my religious days was still hanging out. This programming ran deep. It runs deep for all of us.

I began writing about each experience one by one. How, in high school, I was pimped out by another girl, which felt super shameful. How a guy in high school gave me a ride home from a late night of work and sexually assaulted me. I pretended like I was asleep, hoping he would stop. I didn't know how to speak up for myself, and I thought if I spoke up and told him no, I would be in trouble. How I so badly wanted to be accepted and loved that I had sex with a guy who wasn't even attractive to me. He was just popular, and I thought having sex with him would make me popular, which in my mind equated to love. And at some point, something shifted, and I started having sex on my terms. I liked it, and it was fun, I wanted more, but just thinking about that made me feel guilty and shameful. No one had ever said that sex could be fun and feel good. Everything that had been relayed to me was the opposite.

With each experience I relived, more shame and guilt came to the surface. I could feel the shame in my body, and it felt incredibly uncomfortable. I realized these feelings of shame were still so overwhelming. I sat staring out the window of my office, realizing that even though I'd been writing about all these experiences and memories, I still hadn't processed them. It occurred to me that I'd never even told my therapists about some of these sexual experiences. At the time, I felt too ashamed to let them out into the light. When these sexual experiences happened, I didn't know what to do with them, so I put them in my box and closed the lid. End of story. But it wasn't. The unprocessed emotions were lying in wait for me.

Since I was recalling all these old traumas all at once, my body thought it was right back in the middle of it. I don't think it knew the difference between what was going on in my thoughts and what was happening in real life. It was like a dump truck had pulled up and unloaded all these emotions in my body. My system was going haywire. My belly had been seriously swollen for the entire week of writing about this, yet my body felt tight and contracted. It also occurred to me I hadn't been pooping like I normally do. My body had such a tight grasp on the emotions and trauma that I was bringing back up, it literally wasn't letting go. It was trying to protect me. I had to let go. I cried harder than I've cried in a long time. When we open ourselves up to doing this kind of healing work, our body is right there with us. It's not just our mind that's doing the work. Our body is an incredibly smart reactive being, responding to our thoughts and emotions.

As hard as it was and for how long it took, the way the healing happened was perfect. I trusted my intuition. I trusted the process. It unfolded exactly as it was supposed to. The revealing and healing had to happen in its own way and at its own pace. If I hadn't allowed the emotions of the unhealed wounds to come through, I wouldn't have gotten to the bottom of the box. The unfolding and healing were going to happen whether I held on tight or I let go.

The profound imprint the very first act of abuse left in my psyche has been lifelong. That first act created dark secrets and the belief that I was unlovable. And because I thought I was unlovable, I was doing everything I could to get love. Love is the most basic raw need humans have. We all want to be loved. And if that meant I dressed a certain way to get attention, I was going to do it. If I had to act a certain way to potentially bring love to me, done. Somewhere in my beliefs, I thought maybe getting pimped out was going to get me a boyfriend and he might love me. I was so desperate to feel love, I was going to do whatever it took to get it. When we have an unfillable void inside of us, nothing externally will ever fill it until we heal it. And that takes work. Here's what was actually true: I was loved. I had lots of people around me who loved me; I just couldn't feel it.

Even though I'd uncovered a major piece of why I carried this shame and why I had these patterns, something still lingered at the bottom of my box that I wasn't claiming. I dug deeper still. In order to feel guilt and shame about an event, we have to think we've played some part in the experience, even if it seems like we don't have any responsibility for what happened. If I was feeling guilt and shame, where and for what did I feel a sense of responsibility? What wasn't I taking responsibility for? I began questioning myself. Where was I in denial of my own responsibility? In the recesses of my mind, did I think I'd been flirting too much and thus deserving of these bad experiences? Was I dressed too provocatively? Did I want these sexual experiences to happen to me? The answer is yes! To all of it! I did play a part in all of this, even if it was completely unconscious.

However, saying yes that I played a part in this is a fine line. When we've been abused and oppressed, over-responsibility is definitely one of the characteristics. Shame and guilt are there because we believe we are responsible for what has happened, even though we're not. Part of healing is taking back that sense of responsibility for another's action while, at the same time, owning our part without going into self-judgment or blame.

Asking myself the question of where I played a part in

all of this takes radical responsibility. It takes listening to the very soft, almost imperceptible whisper of our own truth. It requires us to get out of denial and into acceptance. Being responsible takes humility. That's what I was doing. I was listening to the whispers I'd pushed back for so long and finally putting all my pieces together about why this initial act happened in the first place. Everything we experience here on this planet we've planned out, and everything happens perfectly. Over the years, I've learned to trust and surrender to the guidance I receive. Part of my journey to becoming Tara is wanting to know the truth of why I'm here, the deeper parts of me.

I now have a piece of that answer. I contracted before I came here to have the experience of abuse at a very young age so it would inform my life. My life purpose is to have experienced everything that I have so that I can know the depth of these wounds, feel them, and heal them. I'm here to help others go to their own depths, heal their wounds, and hold compassion with them as they do. I'm here to show how to uncover what's been buried deeply within our psyche so we can make more room for love and compassion.

Shame and guilt sit in our bodies like toxic energy. When we hold onto this shame, it becomes too much and wants out of our bodies; it starts to leak out. We try to get rid of our shame and guilt by numbing. We may try to get rid of it by putting it on others. We tell someone, "Shame on you" or "You should feel ashamed of yourself," or covertly attempt to make them feel guilty. We judge others, trying to get this shame out of our bodies. We judge others because there's a piece of us that identifies with whatever we're judging and we don't want to look at it ourselves. These are all ways we try to get rid of our own shame that's stored in our bodies.

When we see our shame and guilt, acknowledge it, feel it, and take responsibility for it, then we are truly able to heal it and release it. It's no longer in our body, and we make room for more love. We have more compassion for ourselves and others. This is part of taking radical responsibility for ourselves. Healing these wounds releases the darkness that's inside of us. Releasing all the darkness inside creates a vacuum, and in that vacuum, the darkness is replaced by the light. When we release the darkness, light floods in. Light is love. Love is the Divine Feminine.

Part of my purpose is to awaken the Divine Feminine. And we cannot awaken with the old wounds still unhealed. Not everyone has a contract like mine. I purposefully chose this to happen to me for the greater good so I can know it and teach it. Claiming this about myself is radical responsibility, and anything less than this would be irresponsible on my part. It can seem egoic that I'm claiming all this about myself. Yet I know this is my truth. I'm telling you what I know is true for me. I'm speaking up. It's who I am at the deepest part of me.

For me to be speaking now about my truth is breaking lifelong patterns formed at an early age. I'm showing you all of me, my dark secrets, all of my shame, my guilt. I'm speaking against what most people believe. I'm speaking against the narrative that tells us we come here as third-dimensional beings with no control or say-so about what happens to us throughout our lives, that our lives are one big series of random happenstances. This is not the truth! I believe we all come here to learn lessons and that everything that happens to us is completely purposeful. I believe we are way more complex and intelligent than we are led to believe. This is true for all of us. And I know if you're reading this, you're ready to wake up and see it. You're ready to honor your entire life experience thus far for what it is.

I'm not condoning what happened to me as a little girl. What I'm saying is that I'm owning that this is my path. I chose this thing to happen for me so that I can now do what I'm here to do. Anything less than claiming this isn't me being me. Being me is sharing and owning my entire life experience. Everything that has happened is what has brought me to this moment right now. If I'd kept any of this closed off, shut down, hidden, and silenced, I wouldn't be acting as my full self but still be operating as a victim. This is me awakening to the Divine Feminine. It's me showing you how to take your own radical responsibility and become you.

I didn't come here to play small. I came here to be big in the world. When we can claim our truth, the truth of seeing everything about ourselves for what we are—our shame, our guilt, our truth of why we came here and own it—that is being in our power. It's being sovereign. Being sovereign means we know ourselves and what we need on a very deep level. We don't need anyone to tell us what to do or who we are. We know what we came here for, and we know what we're doing.

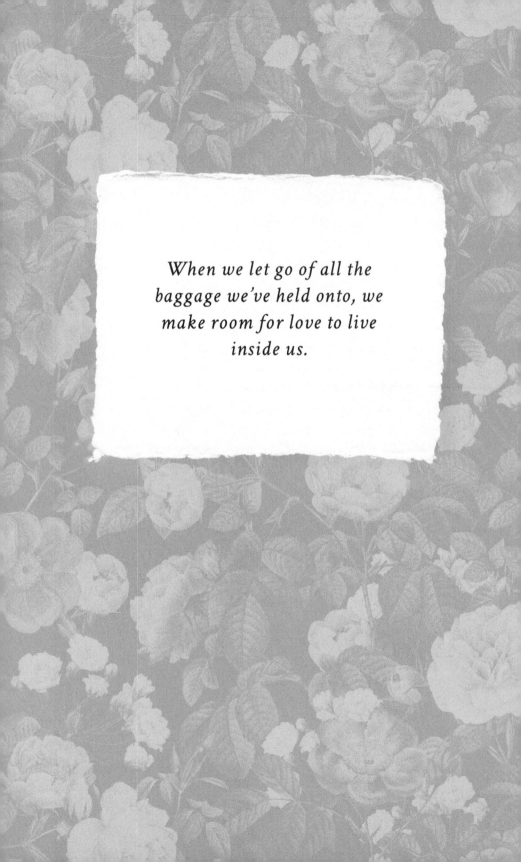

When we let go of all the
baggage we've held onto, we
make room for love to live
inside us.

6

EMBODYING

My body belonged to everyone but me. Or that's what my dark secret had me believe. It instantly taught me that my body was no longer mine. I became afraid of looking any way other than what was expected of me. I was afraid that if I didn't look a particular way or do certain things, you'd take your love away from me. I was afraid you'd decide I wasn't good enough to be your friend. My inner child was deeply wounded.

These wounds showed up in body image issues that lasted most of my life. These secrets I held were a key to a door that had been closed and locked for more than fifty years. Opening this door held pieces to my own puzzle that I didn't realize were missing. Now that I've unlocked it and seen what's there, I'm not afraid to see the rest. The pieces of my puzzle are falling together. Until this point, I didn't have all the information to fully heal and make sense of my life. Facing the shame of my sexual abuse and how it played out in my life led me to be curious about my constant obsession with my body and how I looked. I wondered if this was connected and what else was hidden that I wasn't aware of.

I'd recently taken a self-help course, and one of the areas of focus for me was around my weight and my belly. I wanted to know more about the constant battle going on down there. What was with my decade-plus struggle with food allergies? Why was it so important to me to have a flat belly? During this course, I decided to have a conversation with my belly, which lasted for days and led me on a journey of conversation.

I started with, "Hi, Belly, what's going on in there?"

She responded, "Hi, Tara, I've been suppressing the unhealed emotions you've stuffed down here. We've been holding onto these emotions for as long as we can remember. Let's talk about the battle down here in your belly. The turmoil that rests in here is from the emotions you have stuffed during your childhood, your adult life, and your marriage. You have stuffed everything down here. All your feelings you didn't know what to do with, they're here. All your deep desires that got repressed, they're here. All your concerns that went unheard, they're here. All the love you wanted to give and receive and didn't, it's in here. This is where you've put it all: in your belly. And over the years, on top of all that, you've stuffed us full with food, alcohol, and drugs. You've numbed us severely. We've wondered if we would ever see the light of day. Are you ready for us to come out? We'd love to be seen and heard and validated for the emotions we are. There's a lot of us here."

For as long as I can remember, I've been preoccupied with my weight and the size of my body, never feeling good enough. Growing up in a Catholic grade school, our uniform was a plaid pinafore dress that did absolutely zero for my blossoming female shape other than make it look plump. The pinafore skirt puckered around my waist so that when I wore the required stiff white oxford shirt underneath it and sometimes shorts for gym class, I looked like a starched, fluffy ball of green and blue plaid. The uniform was uncomfortable, and I didn't feel good about myself. I was self-conscious every day.

As a young girl, around 9 or 10, I remember going to our old male family pediatrician for a check-up. I still viscerally remember sitting in his office on the paper-covered exam table. The room smelled sterile. He wore a white doctor's jacket that hung open, showing his tie. His stethoscope hung around his neck. He had glasses that sat at the end of his nose and breath that smelled like moth balls. He told me I was gaining too much weight. He told my mom that I'd better lay off the potatoes and bread. My mom didn't question him. She listened to what he said as if it were the gospel truth.

I followed her lead and didn't question it either. I took his word to be the truth. Hearing him say the words "fat" to my mom filled my body with shame and embarrassment. He was telling her I wasn't good enough as I was. I walked out of his exam room that day feeling heavy in my body; I didn't want anyone to see me. I wanted to be invisible so the moms in the waiting room wouldn't look at me and silently judge me for being "fat" and not good enough. I felt terrible.

Occasionally his words still come to me when I eat potatoes and bread, and I just witness them. This was truly the beginning of me becoming aware that the way my body looked affected other people and that people had opinions about my body and felt entitled to share them. His comments about my body unlocked something deep within me. All the judgment and shame he put on me about my body awakened my unconscious childhood trauma. Because, as a little girl, I felt no control over my situation of abuse, my psyche was constantly trying to regain control, and with this trauma being reactivated, my control mechanisms came back. Even though I'd locked up all the feelings I didn't know what to do with at the time of the abuse, they were still there. I didn't know how to manage all these suppressed feelings and experiences. Being in control was one way to divert the unwanted feelings, and it started with food.

By the time I got to high school, I began looking at myself with a new filter. My high school uniform was much the same as my elementary school one, only the skirt colors were red and blue and the pinafore top was removed. The skirt was still pleated, and it still puckered. I began looking at other girls with a new filter. They were all sorts of shapes and sizes, and I became extremely aware of the differences. I judged them by how they looked. I began putting them in categories of skinny and fat. I started paying attention to the girls who were "fat" and observing how they were treated, not only by students but also by teachers. Students who were bigger received different treatment than the kids who were skinny. I watched how the "skinny" girls were treated, and I noticed they got better treatment, had different friend groups, and seemed happier.

Having this new awareness and wearing the puckered pleated uniform skirt every day made me feel less than great. My self-confidence started waning. My mind was forming new beliefs that would continue throughout my life—beliefs that told me skinny was better; skinny would get me love and acceptance; skinny would bring me the life I wanted; and best of all, skinny would erase the dark secrets I carried. My mind began working overtime to figure out how to gain control. It didn't take long.

As a freshman in high school, the hungry feeling in my belly started showing itself to me as if for a purpose. When I was hungry, something deep within me told me I was in control. Almost like I had one up on the world. It was another secret I had; only this time, I chose it. I would go long periods of time seeing how little I could eat to keep that hunger feeling in my belly. It felt good to me. It gave me a temporary sense of control in my seemingly out-of-control life. The hunger feeling was constant in my belly, and in my mind, that was good. I would eat very little, stopping just when the hunger feeling was about to go away. I never ate until I was full, only enough to take the edge off the burning. I liked the way my body was starting to look when I didn't eat much food. My belly was flat. I thought a woman's body was supposed to be small and have a flat tummy. My mom modeled this to me. She was small and had a flat tummy. It was much like what I thought in high school. If my belly was flat, that must have meant I was getting skinny. And skinny equaled love.

When I went down the road of anorexia, I was trying to be seen for something other than "fat." I wanted approval. I wanted attention, but I was depriving myself. I thought if I could just get control of my body, everything in my life would be better. So, I withheld food from my body. My young teenage mind wasn't able to process the depth of what was actually going on in my unconscious mind. For one to have the desire to deprive themselves of food, of nourishment, there must be deep, unseen, and unhealed wounds. And at this age, I was unaware of my childhood trauma. All I knew was that I hated the body I was in. I'd been told it was fat. It felt disgusting. I was trying to claw my way out of my body.

But for as much as I hated the body I was in, I was silently screaming to be seen. I thought no one saw me. I wanted to be loved because I thought no one actually loved me. They told me they loved me. They showed me in different ways, but I couldn't feel it. I didn't know how to receive it. It was too dangerous for me to allow love in because, in my mind, it wasn't safe to be seen or loved. I had so many opposing feelings happening at the same time. I couldn't allow myself to receive nourishment because I didn't know how to love myself. If I knew how to receive love, I wouldn't have chosen to starve myself. My trauma was blocking all of it. I didn't realize that what wanted to be seen was my trauma.

My desperate desire to be seen stemmed from the deeper desire for someone to see and know this secret of abuse I held and to still love me anyway. That was at the core of my wanting to be seen. At the time of the abuse, I was told I could never tell anyone or I would be punished. My psyche internalized this to mean I was bad. I wanted to be seen and acknowledged and loved despite this. If I could just not be fat, I would be lovable, and I would get the attention I craved.

At the same time I was starving myself, I remember becoming aware of the news around Karen Carpenter, one of my favorite singers. The news constantly talked about how skinny she was, that her family was concerned about her lack of weight and how she wasn't eating. She was receiving a lot of attention, and it seemed like a lot of love. She was anorexic. Along with being a singer, being anorexic was also an identity for her. I wanted an identity. I was constantly trying to figure out who I was. Something in this whole scene seemed glamorous to me. She was in the spotlight.

On a soul level, I also identified with being in the spotlight, being on stage, being seen all over the world, and bringing joy to people. That soft whisper in my head that kept telling me I was here to do big things and help the world was still making itself known to me. I resonated with it. At the time, I didn't know what I was supposed to do or even what it meant, but the knowingness was always there. It was another secret I held. Part of me thought that if I was going to be in the spotlight too, then my body had to look a certain way. I was young and impressionable. I identified with Karen's persona on stage and thought this was how a famous person looks. I wanted to be seen like she was—glamorous and skinny.

By the time I was 14, I'd been active with this deprivation for more than six months when I heard Karen died from anorexia. That shocked me. I didn't want to die like she did. Something had to change. If I stayed on this course, I was going down a very different road, and I didn't want that.

Growing up, Sunday dinners were always at my grandparents' farmhouse. The Sunday after hearing the news, I remember sitting at the table being very aware of the hunger in my belly. I'd just finished the small amount of food I'd put on my plate, and I knew if I had any more, that burning feeling was going to go away. I sat in my seat, thinking about what I was going to do. I sat with the feelings of desperately wanting to be in control and the feelings of being scared to eat the food in front of me. It was a very surreal place for me to be. If I ate any more food, I would no longer be hungry and no longer be in control. The temptation to stay hungry was strong. Thankfully that day, an invisible force made the decision for me.

My grandma had garden fresh creamed corn in her crock pot, and it was so good, I couldn't pass up seconds. I realized her delicious food was more important to me than staying hungry. It was a turning point for me. I was sad—sad that I wasn't going to have the identity of being anorexic, sad that I wasn't going to be loved, sad that I wasn't going to get the attention I wanted. I relinquished the control feelings I had with the hunger in my belly only to later replace them with feeling stuffed. I slid from one end of the scale to another.

During the summers, I helped my grandma with her very large garden. I loved being out in the Midwest summer sun in the dirt, tending to the garden. My cousins and I would spend hours planting, watering, and picking. After I decided the path of anorexia was too scary for me, I relaxed a bit and realized how much I loved eating all our freshly picked fruits and vegetables. Those dinners were my favorites. And for desserts, my grandma used the fruits we'd picked in pies and cobblers. Apple and peach pie were the best. We had countertops full of desserts. I loved her desserts as much as I loved her dinners. I was teaching myself what it felt like to feel comfortably full again in my body.

One particular Sunday, I'd gone back for a second round of fresh beefsteak tomatoes, cucumber, and onions. My grandpa walked by the table and told me, if I kept eating like that, I was going to weigh as much as his cows out in the field. He laughed like it was funny. I was embarrassed and ashamed to be called out like that again. I felt sad to be told once again that my body wasn't good enough as it was. Why was my body such an issue for men, and why do they feel so entitled to comment about it?

The next week, I'd gone back again for seconds, had a

couple bites, then realized how full I was and couldn't finish the rest. Grandpa walked by me at that moment and told me that I had to eat all the food I put on my plate. He said if I was going to put it on my plate, I was going to eat it, even if I was full. He would not allow me to waste food in his house. I was confused, receiving two different messages from the same man. One week he told me I was going to get fat and I better stop eating so much, and the next he was telling me I had to eat all the food on my plate. Instead of the self-regulation naturally beginning to take place, he told me to keep eating. I finished my plate and felt overly full.

It wasn't any different from growing up in my parents' house. We were told the same thing: that we had to clean up our plates. But since I'd just ended the period of not eating and was once again enjoying food, something in the moment with my grandpa shifted in my subconscious. My brain realized the overly full feeling would mask the other uncomfortable feelings I was having. There was something subtly controlling about overeating, I discovered. When I ate more than I needed, it took my mind off what I was thinking about and brought my awareness to the fullness in my belly. That overly full feeling I was now teaching my body overrode the comfortable satiated feeling I had when I was normally full. Actually, it was just another way of not feeling.

Using our own discernment is self-regulation. It's learning what feels good for us internally despite what's going on outside. It's acting on what feels good to us without the worry of outside sources altering our behavior. It's not being worried about what others will think or how they will act; it's us being able to be us. Most of us are not brought up being encouraged to think for ourselves. Most of us are told what to do, and we do it. Some of us learn it's easier and safer to act according to what we think others will say and how they will respond. We convince ourselves this is how life works. This is the opposite of self-regulation; it's codependency.

Self-regulation is when we learn to take responsibility for our own actions. It's knowing what feels right, acting on it, then adjusting accordingly. If everything works out like we thought, all is well. If it didn't work out like we thought, we think about it, make adjustments, and continue on. In learning how to self-regulate when we don't like how we feel internally, we'll naturally change our external behavior. If we like how we feel, we'll continue this behavior until we're called to reevaluate it and do something else.

The perfect example of this was my grandpa telling me to eat more even when I was full. I wasn't allowed to self-regulate. He didn't care how I was feeling, he had his own agenda, and his agenda was that he was in charge and I would do what he said. Once again, I thought a man was here to tell me what to do, so I listened and obeyed. And I felt ashamed and chubby, and I didn't like it. The voices of men were dominating my mind, dictating how I thought and how I behaved. I was letting their feelings and actions override my own feelings and actions.

As I graduated from high school and started out in the real

world, I wanted to change the way I looked. I wanted to reshape my young adult body into what I thought a woman's body was supposed to look like, still convinced that would bring me love. I continued to believe this was part of a woman's life. I started reading everything I could get my hands on about different ways to eat. Diet options were abundant in the late 1980s and early '90s: The Atkins Diet, Fit for Life, low carb, low fat, calorie counting, cabbage diet, liquid diets, the Zone diet, eating for your blood type. Everyone else was trying to get skinny too. Most of these diet books were authored by men. Men were still telling me how to look. They all had an expert opinion on how to lose weight, and I trusted they all knew what they were doing.

These diets were all about restriction and control; they were about removing certain food groups and controlling what you ate. This control was extremely similar to what I'd experienced and participated in when I starved myself, only now dieting was considered socially acceptable. Now I could get skinny and not have to be anorexic. Dieting became another identity for me.

Alongside trying all these different diets, I started exercising. I loved running. It kept me fit, it kept my tummy semi-flat, and it allowed me to eat more than normal. If I ate too much at night, I'd just run a little extra the next day. During this experimentation time, I started dating my now husband. He showered me with compliments. He was always telling me I looked good. Eventually he said the words "I love you," and I thought, *Finally! A man loves me. I've done exactly what I wanted to do, get love by being skinny. Now my life will be perfect despite my dark secret.*

Before I got married, even though I was anorexic and concerned about how I looked, my clothes size and scale numbers meant nothing to me. The control wasn't about the numbers, it was about how I felt in my clothes. However, the moment my soon-to-be-husband said I love you, my psyche latched onto everything I'd become to make myself loveable. In my mind, the size 4 and my current weight equaled love. The control had shifted. It was now about the numbers. I was no longer willing to starve myself, but I was willing to control the numbers on the scale and the size of my waist.

Once we were married, George went into the military. It was a new world to me. The new and seasoned wives around me said it was my job to support my husband at all costs. I thought maintaining my size and weight would reflect well on him. If his wife looked good, then he must be good. I worked hard maintaining my size. Even when I had babies, it didn't take me long to get right back to where I needed to be. I was going to do whatever it took to keep his love.

Though he told me often how much he loved me and how great I looked, the feeling of being loved never lasted long for me. It was always fleeting. His words were never enough. I believed I was only lovable if I looked good. Even though I was no longer starving myself, I hadn't learned to receive the love and nourishment I deeply wanted. My constant search for love was insatiable. I thought the better I was, the more he would love me. I would make sure the house was extra clean, thinking he would love me more. I would buy something sexy to wear, hoping he would love me more. I would have extra sex and give him more compliments. I would boost his ego, hoping that because he felt better about himself, he would share some of that with me. I did anything I could for another hit of the feeling. I was always searching for the unattainable thing that I couldn't feel. I could see the signs of love, but no matter how many times he told me, it would never fill my void. It was still too dangerous for me to allow love in because, in my mind, I was flawed, and so the feelings of love he tried to share with me didn't last.

Several years into our marriage, I decided to become a fitness instructor. I was already fit and I liked exercise, so this seemed like a natural next step for me. As soon as I started teaching classes, I discovered I liked being in front of groups. I felt comfortable as a leader in the spotlight. While teaching classes, I also started training for bodybuilding. There were a couple women at the gym training for a competition, and they looked great. I wanted to look that great, so I started training too. The more I trained, the smaller I became. It didn't take long before I needed a new pair of jeans and went shopping. As I was trying on jeans, I realized I was fitting into a size 0-2. I was elated. I thought to myself, *does that say 0-2? Not only am I buying these because they look great on me but they're telling me I'm perfect! I'm a size 0!* I thought, *I have arrived! Now everyone can love me because I'm a perfect size zero.* Just knowing I could fit into a 0-2 made me feel self-important inside. It gave me another identity. I was the skinny girl. I was George's skinny hot wife.

I thought I was a trophy wife. And everyone loves a trophy.

In truth, there was hardly any of me left to love. In my attempt to have the perfect loveable female body, I had whittled away my soft feminine curves and was left with a straight, hard, and masculine form. I couldn't see this for myself. All I could see was skinny. This is what I thought a female body looked like. I was rejecting my femininity. I was unconsciously rejecting who I was. Unless I was a certain size, I wasn't good enough and I wasn't lovable. The voices of others throughout my life who had found a permanent position in my mind were reminding me that to be loved, I needed to keep my body fit, in shape, skinny, and tight. My mind was telling me I had to get as small as possible to be loved. I was disappearing to be seen.

This facade represented a false sense of control in a life over which I had almost no control. I was deeply wounded. I thought the only way for me to outwardly project self-confidence and control was to portray a great body and a great life. In my delusional trauma-filled mind, I thought, since everyone told me how good I looked, it meant I had my life all together. I looked great, I had lots of friends, I was always happy, and I was in control. This in-control, great life meant love, and everyone could see how great my life was. I was certain if I let any of what I'd achieved go, people would stop loving me. If I didn't look this way, they would see that I was actually unlovable and didn't know what I was doing at all. I was always one step away from being found out.

When I went into a dressing room to buy clothes, anxiety

coursed through my body. I was nervous because I thought, in some crazy delusional way, I'd gained weight and the number on the clothes would have changed. And if they were larger, that meant I was unlovable. George would be ashamed of me. Women would no longer like me or want to be my friend. Men wouldn't want to have sex with me. My whole world would crumble. I would have hit rock bottom and would have to claw my way back up. I could never allow this to happen. Being small wasn't safe because that size might go away at any time. Being bigger definitely wasn't safe either because that wouldn't bring me love. I wasn't safe anywhere in my body.

As I've grown older, I've thought surely there is more to life than this. I wanted to get off the crazy train. It's only been in recent years of uncovering my trauma that I've begun seeing the lasting effects of that early abuse. Unconsciously, I thought my body wasn't mine, that I didn't deserve love, that I was inherently bad, that all men wanted from me was sex, that I had to be a certain size to be loveable. The list is actually pretty long. Essentially, I believed if everyone loved me, I was safe. Receiving love is one of our core needs as a human beings, and that's what I spent my life looking for.

Uncovering all these old beliefs made me realize that keeping my weight and body at a certain size was not only a way to control myself but also a way to control others. I wasn't allowing anyone, including myself, to have an experience of the real me. It was a version of me. I wasn't giving my husband the chance to know me any other way. I didn't know myself any other way. I wasn't allowing him to expand his emotional capacity to love me any differently. I wasn't evolving. I was keeping myself in a tight box, which meant I was trying to keep his emotions about me in a tight box. I wasn't giving either of us a chance to emotionally grow. He liked the way I looked; I liked that he liked it. I was pleasing him, and I was controlling our situation. That's what a codependent and people pleaser does. It's an exhausting way of life.

I knew there must be another way. And there was. The next step scared the shit out of me. In the recesses of my mind, I knew starting down a path of curiosity was going to rock my world. I know that we don't live in a vacuum. When we make changes, it affects everyone around us. Others will react to how we are changing. They'll want to know why we're doing life differently. And most of the time, change is met with resistance, big time! Did I think I had what it took to make these changes? My answer to myself was, *I think so. I hope so because the way I'm living now can't go on. I don't want to do this anymore.*

Part of learning is also unlearning.

7

CONTROLLING

I started therapy in my early 30s. When I started, I was an enmeshed, toxic, codependent people pleaser with a history of toxic relationships. I had zero idea who I was or that all this existed within me. Well, I thought I knew who I was. I thought I was a runner and an aerobics instructor, I was skinny, and I was a mom and George's wife. I thought I was really happy in all that.

Starting therapy was like going to school and learning a whole new way to live. Everything was new to me. I learned new ways to look at situations. I learned new ways to talk. I learned what was working in my life and what wasn't. I started questioning what I believed in and why. And it was all incredibly scary. It was rocking the entire foundation that I'd built my life upon. My foundation was beginning to crumble, and to say I was scared is an understatement. I was terrified that at any given moment, everyone who loved me would take their love back because I was starting to do life a different way. Making changes causes a ripple. Something deep inside me told me that once I started down this road, there was no going back. I knew I would never be able to unknow the things I would reveal to myself doing this work.

With my first therapist, I was constantly making excuses for how everyone in my family acted. I thought I was in denial when, in reality, I was super ashamed. At a point in childhood, I started realizing our family operated differently than others, but I couldn't bring that up with my mother, fearing it would cause more problems than I could manage. We didn't talk about all the arguments in our family and how I thought things were wrong, and we certainly didn't tell other people about it. I referred to the yelling that went on in my family as "we're a passionate bunch." When I got married, I followed the same unwritten rules.

Initially, I thought therapy would help me with the crazy thoughts starting to make their way into my consciousness. I began to wonder if the way I'd lived my life up to this point might not be normal. I was starting to wonder if the way I'd been raised was different from how others were raised. My crazy thoughts were doing a number on me. I was having anxiety and diarrhea, and I wasn't sleeping.

I thought a therapist could help me sort this out. This was a radical step for me because, according to my parents and grandparents, only crazy people went to therapy. My family believed that if you can't work out your own problems, then you've got some serious issues. The irony of this is not lost on me.

Toward the end of my initial session, my therapist asked me what I wanted to achieve. I replied something along the lines of "I had a blow-up with my mom and wanted to learn how to change the way she acted toward me." She suggested we start meeting several times a week for the first several months to get things rolling. *She must really like me and think I'm a good person,* I thought. This was completely validating to the part of me that thought I was unlovable. My therapist, a trained professional, liked me enough and cared about me enough that she wanted to see me this often. But really, I knew it would only take me a couple sessions and I'd be good to go.

Each time I would get to her office and sit in the waiting room, I'd look at the other people around me and think to myself, *they must be really messed up. I'm only here for a tiny issue with my mom. They're probably the crazy ones. Poor them.* I had no idea how deep in self-denial I was. It never occurred to me that I'd given her serious signs in that initial session that I was a complete codependent, people-pleasing mess with no boundaries who needed serious help.

During our sessions, I started learning about words I'd never heard before, like *codependency, enmeshment, toxic relationships, dysfunctional, boundaries.* My therapist started helping me reframe some of my thought processes. She started shining a light on the way I behaved and the way others around me behaved. She started using words like *healthy behavior,* suggesting to me that mine wasn't.

She started showing me how my behaviors around food,

exercise, and eating were obsessive. We talked about how I saw myself in the mirror and what I thought I looked like. We talked about body image and what body dysmorphia was. I understood what she was telling me, but it wasn't sinking in. She didn't understand that for me to be me, I had to know what I ate, count calories, or restrict myself if I thought I had previously eaten too much. I could slightly see how I might be obsessed around my eating, but I didn't believe I actually was. I thought my behavior was pretty normal. Anyone who wanted love like I did was going to maintain a specific body size. And since I was no longer anorexic and starving myself, it felt fine to me to be restrictive and aware of what I was eating. She just didn't understand this was the way I had to be.

She also asked me if I'd ever chewed my nails or if I'd ever had eye twitches. I was astounded she asked me these questions because the answer to both was yes. How did she know? For weeks we'd been talking about what obsessive behaviors were and how they are used as a form of control. She kept giving me examples of these behaviors in other people, hoping I would make the connection with myself. When I didn't, she actually used the term *obsessive-compulsive behavior* and listed my behaviors in the same sentence. I had a momentary shift in perspective, a nanosecond of a thought that she might be onto something.

And then, as fast as it came into my awareness, it left again. How could she think I had OCD? I wasn't obsessive or compulsive. And I was happy. I figured people with OCD were unhappy, so I couldn't be one of them. I was in control and getting everything I wanted. I was utterly unaware I was caught in a cycle. This is just how I did life.

I didn't chew my nails anymore because now I had fake nails, so we can check that one off the list. And my eye twitching only happened sporadically, and it had mainly happened when I was young. I doubted her abilities. I thought this might be the actual proof that my family was right: therapists really were quacks. But because I'd already paid for so many sessions, I decided to listen to what she was telling me and wondered if there was more to this.

This journey of therapy and learning about myself and learning the concepts she was teaching me were complete eye-openers. Not only was I learning that the way I was raised wasn't healthy, but I learned the way I was raising my children also wasn't healthy. Apparently, those crazy thoughts were onto something. I had to relearn everything I'd known up to that point. I was rewiring my brain. She started teaching me how we attach meaning to what we believe. Sometimes we attach our entire self to what we believe and make our beliefs our identity.

She taught me that beliefs are fluid; we can change them at any time. Just because my parents believed in something didn't mean I had to. I could make my own choices on what I believed. I could choose to believe in a different religion if I wanted to. Or, I didn't have to believe in religion at all. I could choose to have a different political view than my family or step away from political views altogether. It was completely up to me. She was blowing my mind. I didn't know I could make my own choices like this.

At moments throughout my life, I would secretly think, in a perfect world, *wouldn't it be great to be able to do and say what I wanted to without worrying about others making fun of me, shaming me, or judging me?* My submissive brain quickly popped these thoughts, reminding me I didn't live in that perfect world and it wasn't the narrative I was living in. According to my therapist, we either believe that the world is a really safe and supportive place and anything is possible or we believe life is scary, we can't trust others, we can't count on others, and to get love, we have to act a certain way. She told me I could change all this, but it was up to me to do it. And in order to do that, we would have to go back to where these beliefs originated. I would have to look at why I believe what I believe and behave the way I behave.

As scary as it was for me to explore more questions about growing up and reveal more of my childhood to her, I did. But I could only access as much as I was ready to access. I still felt like I was betraying the unwritten laws and rules of my family. It felt clandestine to talk about our family with her, but I was more curious to discover what other patterns I'd grown up with could be changed. The changes I was being called to make felt scary. I was afraid of being shamed for trying to change myself and affecting the way our family had been working since before I was born. I was overwhelmingly afraid of being shamed by them.

The more we talked and the more I shared, the more I realized I was raised in a narcissistic environment. Another new term for me. My curiosity on this topic was insatiable. I began reading as many books as I could get my hands on. The more I read, the more my early years began to make sense. A narcissist takes up a lot of space, which doesn't leave much room for others. They need to be seen constantly. To make them feel good, they need everyone around them to agree with them and share the same opinions. They don't like to be argued with or challenged; they manipulate and coerce to be in control. They become bullies, they make fun of us, they manipulate us, they control us, they abuse us, they silence us. They need constant adoration at the expense of everyone else. This shed tremendous light on the habits and behaviors I'd adopted over the years and why I'd become a people pleaser.

Being raised in this environment, I was constantly trying to guess what others around me were thinking or what their response would be to my behaviors. I was always trying to be one step ahead. I was constantly trying to predict the future, which is not always possible. Trying to constantly guess others' behaviors caused me a ton of anxiety growing up, and anxiety needs an outlet. As a kid, I didn't know what to do with this anxiety, so I started biting my nails and my eyes twitched. My mom took me to the doctor to find out why my eyes were twitching. My vision was fine, and the doctor told her this is usually caused by stress and anxiety.

On the way home, she asked me what stress I thought I had

in my life. I lied and told her none. I knew I had anxiety, but I wasn't willing to rock the boat and speak up. Lying became second nature to me because telling the truth could get me in trouble and shamed. I'd learned the truth wasn't what people wanted to hear. At this point in my life, I had yet to unearth the memory of my early childhood abuse, which had been a source of unknown anxiety and where I first learned it was safer to lie. This pattern of lying had become normal to me. The truth would cause arguments. I avoided arguments. I wanted love.

For people pleasers, something happens early in our lives to make us think we're unlovable (cue: the root of low self-esteem), and we conclude that pleasing others is the only way to get love, any love. We are constantly trying to maintain a safe and non-threatening environment, so we frequently alter our words and behaviors to make sure those around us love us. This need for safety and belonging trumped my other desires and needs. I thought my needs and desires were unimportant and continually put myself last, which meant my needs went unmet so others would be happy and feel safe. Thinking of everyone else first got me what I wanted: love and acceptance. I was constantly looking outside myself for recognition and love. I was only seen when others felt seen. I was only validated when others felt good about themselves and my behavior. I was validated for who everyone around me was teaching me to be, a people pleaser.

When we're codependent people pleasers, all of our validation comes from the outside, not the inside. I looked to others to tell me what to wear, how to act, what to say, how to look, how to behave, what to eat, and where to go. I outsourced thinking for myself and didn't trust my own thoughts or desires, my mind, or my body. It was too scary to go within to see what felt good for me. What felt good for me might contradict someone else's wants and needs. My internal system had been denied and shut down long ago. I was more worried about everything going on around me than taking care of myself.

My therapist began showing me this old way of validation wasn't healthy. As children, my siblings and I would usually be punished and shamed any time we did something that was considered wrong or inconsiderate. And if we'd done something really big, like getting pregnant before marriage, these actions were ignored, denied, or brushed swiftly under the carpet. I learned that as long as no one saw our shame and wrongdoings, no one could judge us. We kept the same perfect outward persona that everything was great and no one was the wiser. At any given moment, our whole house could be filled with screaming arguments and falling apart inside. The doorbell would ring, and an instant unspoken rule demanded that everyone put on their best face and pretend nothing was wrong. Everything was shoved under the carpet, and we put on our happy faces.

Growing up this way was always confusing to me. *Why couldn't people see us when we were mad or having disagreements? What was wrong with that? Didn't other people get mad too? Why were we only letting them see some parts of us?* This made me sad. I wasn't being seen for all of me. The adults around me didn't know what to do with anger, including their own. If I expressed anger, the adults would get angry right back at me, completely invalidate my anger (I was probably just tired or hungry), or make me feel ashamed of it, so I learned anger wasn't good. In fact, it made me bad, unlovable, and shameful. I learned to shove anger way down. I would keep it under the surface, letting it fester until I couldn't hold back any longer, and then I would explode at the simplest thing. And as soon as I did, I felt ashamed of myself.

Growing up, you may have heard the phrase: "You should be ashamed of yourself." I heard it all the time from various people around me. I think it was the go-to phrase adults used when they didn't know what to say or how to handle a situation. Most of the adults around me didn't know how to listen or show me how to validate myself or ask me questions about how I felt. They told me how I should feel.

Consequently, when my children were young, I did exactly the same thing with them. I didn't know how to do anger, so I wouldn't allow them to be mad. I didn't show them how to look within to see how they actually felt. I didn't teach them about the multitude of feelings they could be feeling. I didn't teach them how to decide for themselves how they wanted to feel. I'd learned to look externally for how you're supposed to act and feel. See what everyone else is doing and just follow the crowd.

As people pleasers, we do NOT strike out on our own and proclaim ourselves worthy of living our own life exactly how we want to live it. We aren't in touch with how we really feel. To be in touch with these feelings means we are attuned with ourselves, and that's just not us. People pleasers certainly don't get angry. It's kind of our code. And because we don't get angry, we use substances or behaviors to numb our anger. We numb the rest of our feelings. We numb what we really want to say. People pleasing itself is a form of numbing. It takes us far away from our center. It can be a big journey to get back.

Until therapy, it wasn't safe for me to look inside. I held too much shame in there, and no one around me held a safe container for me to feel all the big emotions I'd never really felt. The first time my therapist asked me how I felt about a situation, I would respond with "mad." She asked me to go deeper. I didn't know what she meant by "go deeper." I thought she was looking for a specific answer, the right answer, and I didn't know what that was. I didn't realize she wanted to know how I really felt.

Up to this point, it had been comfortable for me to push my feelings aside and ignore them. I was afraid of upsetting others. Identifying and acknowledging my feelings still felt like I was being a traitor to those closest to me. I learned that suppressed anger and resentment were a major cause of my anxiety. People around me weren't appreciating how much of myself I was sacrificing so they would be happy. Because I was trying to keep the peace, I stuffed all my feelings inside. With nowhere to go, they created anxiety.

The adult me sitting in my therapist's office knew she

would likely not be upset with me if I revealed my true feelings, but the still wounded little girl in me was gun shy and didn't trust. However, I recognized that I'd trusted her this far, and I was curious what she would show me next. So, she taught me how to go within and ask myself how I really felt. It took me a while to figure it out. I'd been so used to denying my feelings I thought there were only a handful to choose from. I only knew mad, sad, happy, or afraid. I didn't know that at any given moment, we were allowed to feel many different feelings all at once, even if they contradicted each other. Some of the feelings I identified with I didn't know I was allowed to feel, especially anger.

As silly as it sounds, therapy taught me how to do anger. But it took me a long time not to feel ashamed for it. I felt terrible, clumsy, and self-conscious when I tried to let my anger out. All my life, I'd been told I wasn't angry. I went from one end of the spectrum to another, trying to learn how to be angry. I felt scared that others would get mad at me if I was mad. Once I'd learned that it was okay to be angry and to express it when it was present, my therapist taught me how to get curious about my anger. I learned to ask myself leading questions to discover if I was angry or if it might be something deeper. I didn't realize that anger was the front man for hundreds of other underlying feelings.

Then, one day, she threw me a curve ball. She asked me how I wanted to feel. What do you mean, "How do I want to feel?" I said. No one had ever asked me that before. My brain immediately insisted that what I wanted didn't matter and that she was crazy for asking me this question. Going within to see what I wanted meant I had to start trusting myself again. I'd forgotten long ago how to fully and completely trust what I knew to be true. I learned to default to others. It took many, many sessions for me to think of myself as important enough to decide how I wanted to feel. I was still constantly saying yes so that I wouldn't let anyone down, which often left me feeling resentful. I didn't know it was within my power to change this. I thought this was the hand I was dealt.

As we discussed all this, it started to become clear that I didn't have any boundaries. As people pleasers, most of us don't even know what boundaries are. We're so enmeshed with those around us that we don't know where we stop and they start. It makes us feel bad and guilty to set boundaries because we're worried about how the other person will feel if we do. We don't know how to let them have their own feelings and trust we'll be okay with whatever they are.

When I started setting boundaries, I was still feeling so much anxiety, maybe even more than before I started therapy, because I was doing life differently now. Setting boundaries meant I had to start thinking for myself, claiming myself, feeling my feelings, and deciding how I wanted to feel. It meant I was putting myself before others. It was affecting my relationships. I could no longer predict how others were going to act, and to me, this was completely out of my control. My parents, husband, and children were feeling the effects of my shifting.

I was feeling the effects of my shifting. Everyone wanted to argue with me; they wanted to know why I thought it was so important to change myself. No one liked what I was doing to the family system. I was changing the way it had worked for decades. My new ways of thinking, believing, and acting were butting up against the rest of my family, who were still subscribing to the old ways. They saw me as creating chaos. They thought I was creating arguments and drama. Nobody knew how to handle this new me.

When I started saying no in my marriage and voicing different opinions than what George held, it really rocked the boat. I learned the word *no* is an entire sentence in and of itself. I could just say *no*. I didn't have to explain. This was petrifying. At first, when I would use the word *no*, my voice shook, I wasn't convincing. Up to this point, I agreed with almost everything he said and wanted. Me changing myself was making him angry. I started standing up for myself. I stopped trying to smooth things over. I started allowing myself to be angry and allowing a lot of other emotions to flow through. He didn't know what to do or how to handle the situation, so he got angry. He would storm out of the house. We'd go to bed without resolving our differences.

I was becoming un-meshed, and that can be painful for both parties. My husband didn't have the tools that I was learning and was stuck in not knowing how to express himself adequately. Being in this new territory was painful for me, and I was severely disturbing the peace. I felt scared. I felt guilty because I was causing more arguments in the house and now the kids were affected. I felt like a little kid who was doing something she wasn't supposed to be doing, but it also felt liberating.

I was going within and learning to trust myself, asking myself how I wanted to feel rather than how they wanted me to feel. I was learning to say *yes* to things I wanted. I was slowly beginning to think and act for myself. Up to this point, I'd only known external validation. Setting boundaries and feeling angry, and all these other new emotions I was feeling, was a great place for me to start unlearning my people-pleasing skills. Part of learning is also unlearning.

As people pleasers, there are still times we want to look outward for validation and put others first. It's our default. And it doesn't occur to us that all this validation and love is already inside us. No one's ever told us that, and if they did, we might hardly be able to conceive of it. Now, when I find myself seeking external validation, I recognize it, get curious about why I'm looking externally, and then gently guide myself back to me. Learning this new way to do life meant I was slowly changing the way I acted and reacted with my family.

Now when I have a conversation with my kids or my family, we talk through how we feel internally. We validate those initial feelings no matter what they are. We aren't here to tell others how they are supposed to feel or not feel. We're not here to make others feel bad or guilty. And we're definitely not here to judge others' experiences. This journey we're on is specific to us and no one else. It is, first and foremost, about us. We are here to experience and feel everything for ourselves first. If we are constantly worried about what everyone around us thinks about us, we'll never have the opportunity to decide how or what we think. Worrying about what everyone else thinks takes us off our own course and in a different direction away from our joy. When we're constantly thinking about what other people are going to think, we can't find our center.

Knowing who we are is how we find our center. To get to this place of knowing, we have to see all the darkness that's been hiding by shining a light on what we've kept hidden. Working on all this gradually began bringing my stuff out of the darkness and into the light. We know ourselves when we can identify our feelings and are comfortable expressing them. We know ourselves when we have faith that we can uncover our own dark secrets, no matter how long it takes us.

It's taken me years of work to put myself first and to stop reading the room, trying to guess what's going to happen next. I'll tell you, people pleasing dies hard. I'm still working on it. I still find moments where I give myself away in order to keep the peace. The independent and autonomous woman in me always wants to speak up and call a spade a spade, and the old people pleaser wants to sweep it under the carpet and not stir the pot. Most of the time, I have the strength and courage for it, but sometimes I don't. And in those moments when I don't feel strong, I remind myself to have compassion for my journey. Standing in my authentic truth is not natural yet. I have to think about it. My therapist reminded me it's a life-long practice I'd be practicing for the rest of my life.

The irony of being a people pleaser or codependent is that we're acting and behaving this way simply because we desperately want people to love us. We want everyone to unconditionally love everything about us. Yet we've never loved ourselves that way. We want others to see us for who we really are, not all the pretenses we've put up. We want people to love what's deep inside us, but we're too afraid to show them.

And the truth is this: no one is more attractive, more sexy, more alluring, and more deeply lovable than when they are in their authentic sovereign self, when they are thinking for themselves, doing what they want to do, having authority over themselves, knowing who they are, loving themselves, and taking responsibility for themselves. It is up to us to discover and root into this place within us; no one else can do it for us. And we can't tap into our own depth until we're ready. Often something external happens in our lives that wakes us up. The argument I had with my mom was my tipping point. I wasn't sure what needed to shift; I just knew things were out of balance and thought she needed to shift, not me. This is when we internally know it's time to dive in and make a change. That's when we are on our way to becoming our most loving, lovable, authentic version of us. That's when we will begin to know the depths of who we are.

When we can claim our own wounding and heal it, the effects of our healing ripple out to everyone.

8

MOTHERING

At 19, I moved out of my parents' house and in with my boyfriend. I was trying to separate myself from them. I wanted to establish my own life. I thought I was going to play house. I thought if I pretended to play the role of wife for him, he would love me forever and ever. I'd shifted my focus from needing and wanting love from my parents to needing and wanting love from my boyfriend.

He was an addict. He could be mean, abusive, and unpredictable. I thought if I could love him enough, I could save him. As a people pleaser, I always thought I could manipulate others' behavior and turn them around. And turning them around meant they would love me. If he could just see how much I loved him, he would realize he loved me too, stop all of his addictions, change his ways, and life would be good.

When that didn't happen, I stopped taking my birth control pills without telling him. And got pregnant. I was trying to coerce and manipulate him even more into loving me. This is classic codependency. I was looking for the love I thought was elusive, and I was willing to do almost anything to get it. Even though my upbringing taught me sex out of the sanctity of marriage was wrong and I should be ashamed of myself for being pregnant and unmarried, the desperation to get love from my boyfriend trumped the feelings of shame I knew I would get from my parents.

A few months after getting pregnant, I realized my boyfriend's addictive habits were getting worse. His anger and fits of rage were becoming more frequent. It was time for me to move back to my parents' house and figure out what I was going to do next. This made me anxious. First, I would have to tell them I was pregnant, which went against everything they believed in. Second, I knew they'd ask if I was going to marry him, which was a hard no for me. I knew I couldn't marry him or ever go back to that relationship because going back meant going down a dark road from which I'd most likely never recover. I was being physically and emotionally abused, and I hadn't told them about it. I was ashamed of the abuse because I thought it was all my fault. My programming told me that if I knew better, I would have stopped it, told someone, or left. I did none of those things.

When I told them about the pregnancy (not the abuse), they were shocked, embarrassed, and ashamed of me and told me as much. This is how shame works—if we carry shame about ourselves, we will project it onto others. They were so full of their own shame from their upbringing; my getting pregnant was a projection of the shame they already felt. The dogma they believed in was so strong they couldn't figure out how to make this "right" in their minds.

Abortion was completely out of the question for them because, according to our religion, it was a sin. They talked to me about adoption. But that was out for me too. Something deep within me knew I was supposed to have this child. It was incredibly hard for me to use my voice and say this. I was going against all my religious programming, societal programming, and my parents' programming. I was afraid of what my parents would do. I thought they would boot me out of the house. But I had to speak up. I told them I was keeping the baby. I had to claim what was true for me. At the time, I had no idea the profound effect my first child would have on me; I just knew this baby was meant to be in my life.

Toward the end of my pregnancy, my parents adjusted to the idea of me having a baby, unmarried at 21, and began helping me make preparations. But I was confused. At first, they were so ashamed. What changed for them? This need from my parents to be seen as a perfect and unflawed family ran deeper than I'd ever imagined. They thought we had to present the perfect persona to the outside world in order to be loved, and apparently, now that meant welcoming a child into the world with open arms. Presenting the perfect persona gives us the illusion that no one sees our shame. It's perpetuating our wounds. The generations before me needed healing. I needed healing. Even with my inner knowing that I was to keep this child, I still felt ashamed there was a baby in my belly.

Shame is its own perpetuating cycle. If our parents have shame, they knowingly and unknowingly transfer it to us. They verbally shame us with their words such as "you should be ashamed of yourself" and "shame on you." They give us punishments that make us feel shameful. In an attempt to get rid of their own shame, they transfer it to us. As children, we unknowingly feel the energy of their shame, take it on, and allow it to live in our bodies as if it were our own. With all this shame in our bodies, we feel like we have to hide our feelings. It's a double whammy. We don't have a safe space to express ourselves without judgment. And as a child, we most likely don't know how to put all this into words.

As we grow into adults, we hold all this memory and information in our cells. When we have children, we knowingly or unknowingly transfer this shame to them. I was beginning to see how shame is one of the biggest coercive manipulative behaviors there is, whether we are manipulating our own behaviors or others' so that we can feel good and not feel our unhealed wounds. Shame creates within us guilt, unworthiness, and disconnection from ourselves. We think we're intrinsically bad. We don't think we're lovable. We think we deserve abuse. We become depressed and anxious, and we view the world through this lens of shame. We think we are the shame rather than being able to identify that shame is a feeling we're having.

Most of us aren't aware that shame is a physical feeling in

our bodies. It is pervasive, like a constant itch we can't scratch. Shame is toxic. It can cause all kinds of physical symptoms. It settles in our bodies and can cause disease. Whether we're in denial or just have no desire to tap into what's in there, we're always trying to get rid of that feeling. We try to get rid of the feeling through our addictions. Shame can compel us to drink too much, eat too much or not enough, shop too much, have affairs, gamble, or smoke. And the habits we use to numb our shame often create more shame.

We become angry, cynical, and paranoid; we expect the worst from others, thinking others always have an ulterior motive. All these feelings can become overwhelming, and we might think it's too much to handle. So, we try to project the shame out of our bodies and onto others. We do this by making fun of people, shaming them, verbally attacking them, and controlling and manipulating them so we don't get triggered into feeling our shame. Shame is a constant motivator for our actions or inactions.

Bringing up old stuff to feel and potentially changing is huge. All the stuff we ignore or think we've buried is part of our story. Our story is who we think we are. It's what has happened to us up to this moment in time and what we've made it mean. It's the filter through which we see the world. And my story, my life was full of shame, numbing, addictions, and silence. Unfortunately, until we're ready to see our unhealed shame and feel it and heal it, it will follow us everywhere. It will be present when we lash out at someone. It'll be with us when we feel like a victim. It'll show up when we are full of rage at a seemingly small event. Unhealed shame makes us want to run away from our lives so we presumably won't have to feel it.

The cycle continues through generations until one person knowingly and willingly stops the cycle. I was shamed by my parents, they were shamed by their parents, who were shamed by their parents, and so on. Through my journey of healing and discovery, I was realizing the impact this cycle had on my life. Because of my shame, I became a people pleaser. I had lots of addictions, OCD, anorexia, and low self-esteem. I felt unworthy, had anxiety, and was completely disconnected from myself. Shame had been used in my childhood, my religion, my schooling, in my marriage, and I used it with my children.

During my time away from work, one particular memory with my oldest son continued to come in and out of my awareness. When he was 19, the same age as when I moved out of the house, we made him move out of the house. As soon as this memory would pop up, I'd tell myself it was so long ago that it didn't have any bearing on my life today. But I would wake up at night, and this memory would be the first thing I'd think of, and my body would start aching. I'd have a hard time going back to sleep. When I was out walking or running, the memory would pop into my mind and create a ton of anxiety in my body. I felt like I wanted to crawl out of my skin. And sometimes it felt like deep sadness and grief, like a void I couldn't fill.

I wanted to pretend like it didn't exist. And by pretending

it didn't exist, I was denying it. My heart was starting to have physical pain in it. I would feel heaviness in my chest. I talked to the pain and asked what was going on. I discovered the pain came from disconnecting from this memory, pretending like it didn't exist. So often we fear that if we open our hearts and feel the pain, we won't be able to handle it or that it will never stop. The irony is that by keeping our hearts closed and denying ourselves the memory and the experience to heal it, we experience even greater (and sometimes life-threatening) pain. We numb more and deny more.

When I experienced this pain in my stomach, it would tense up with anxiety. I asked the pain in my stomach to talk to me. As I listened, it told me that it literally couldn't stomach the feelings of guilt and shame anymore and this was just too hard to hold onto. It also told me it held a lot of buried stories and emotions for me to uncover. Years and years of denial were trapped in my belly. The pain was telling me to either let it out and heal it or it was going to get worse. It was time to let it out. I cried. When the memory of booting him out of the house started to surface, I allowed it in. Instead of getting angry and frustrated with the pain it was causing me, I started to feel into it.

I remember the day my son left our house, he didn't have a plan, only that he was going to stay with a friend and his parents until he could figure it out. He had no idea what he was going to do. I felt like I was betraying my child, but I didn't have the courage to say anything. My body was wracked with anxiety all the while I was battling the voice of shame inside me telling me it was time for him to go.

I let none of these feelings see the light of day. I stuffed them. I stayed quiet. I didn't speak. I didn't tell my husband any of the things I thought or felt. I convinced myself I was teaching my son a good lesson in being prepared and the consequences that come when you're not prepared. I told myself I was being a good mom, that I was teaching him to be strong when, in fact, I was doing the opposite. I was teaching him what fear, loneliness, and low self-esteem looked and felt like.

My little whisper, the one I often ignored, tried to tell me that this was the wrong decision. But I ignored it. For me and the sake of the household (so I thought), it was easier to just stay quiet. On one hand, I stayed silent to avoid conflict with my husband. And on the other hand, I stayed silent because I was unconsciously trying to rid myself of my shame. When I told my son it was time to move out of the house, I was literally trying to kick out all my shame. He represented the physical embodiment of this shame, and unbeknownst to me, I would do anything to get rid of the shame in my body. I was making it leave my house.

However, when he moved out, my shame didn't go away. I was utterly torn between thinking I'd done the right thing and feeling like I'd let him down. I didn't speak up for my child; I wasn't his voice and his advocate at a time when he needed me. I chose staying silent over listening to my inner knowing. I felt ashamed to ask for what I wanted, guilty for having a different viewpoint, afraid of what that would mean, and terrified to set boundaries. I kicked him out instead of facing my shame and speaking up. I thought staying quiet meant I didn't have to feel the shame. But it just made the shame worse. Staying quiet meant more peace in the household for everyone else. But staying quiet came at a big cost for me.

In remembering this situation so vividly and allowing it in, now I understand the depths of the shame I was feeling. I began acknowledging to myself that I felt ashamed about what I'd done and what I hadn't done. I began allowing the pain of shame and guilt to surface in my body. I didn't know what to expect. I didn't know how long the pain was going to last. Part of me thought I would become an emotional wreck and wouldn't know how to handle this. But I did it anyway. I allowed myself to cry about it. My tears were full of guilt and anguish. When I was at the pool, I would wear a big sunhat and sunglasses so other people couldn't see me, and I would cry. I would let myself feel this pain in my body. I would go home and sit on my bathroom floor and sob. My bathroom floor became one of my safe places to cry and heal. I was beginning to release the shame and guilt I'd been feeling for years.

I realized the only way to fully release the pain from my body was to talk to my son. If the memory of this particular situation was causing me this much pain, I wondered what had it done to him over the years. My body was shaking at the thought of calling him and talking about how guilty and shameful I felt for everything that had unfolded. I didn't know how the conversation would unfold or how he would receive it. I didn't know if he would hear me or be angry with me. I just knew that it was time to start taking responsibility for myself and my actions, or lack thereof.

I sent him a text asking if we could talk on his next day off. The day came, and I was a nervous wreck. I couldn't eat, my stomach hurt. I was jittery. I sat at my desk, my body shaking. I thought I was going to throw up. I took a deep breath and called him. I confessed to him that when he was 19 and we made him move out, I knew he wasn't fully prepared.

While crying, I said, "I imagined you must have felt scared and lonely and abandoned, not being sure you could fully support yourself. One of my greatest gifts in the world is being a mom, and in that, I let you down. I was wrong. I failed you."

Speaking these words to him brought all my pain to the surface. Continuing felt excruciating.

"When we made you move out, I feel like it severed my relationship with you. I wasn't ready for that. I wasn't done being your full-time mom. I felt like you still needed us, and I cut you off," I said.

After a moment of silence, my son spoke up and said, "I did feel alone and abandoned. I thought it was all my fault."

He felt bad about himself. He sat silent on the phone as I cried more. I couldn't stop. I felt like it was never going to end. All the feelings I'd been having over the last several years were now validated and amplified. Everything I feared he felt was exactly how he felt: alone and betrayed.

Finally, my crying started to slow down. I took deep breaths. The shaking in my body slowed down. As I quieted down, I whispered to him, "Thank you for sitting through this with me. It's so painful to feel all this. My shame is almost unbearable."

I asked him how he felt.

"I don't feel as alone and abandoned anymore. I feel seen. I feel freedom, actually, because you're finally seeing my pain and taking responsibility for your part. I know it took guts for you to call me. Thanks, Mom. I finally feel like I have a safety net underneath me."

In later days, as I processed our conversation and acknowledged the courage it took to speak, I realized how healing it was for me to actually say all these words out loud. Someone else was seeing my shame and guilt, and it was the person to whom I'd caused the pain. I was physically letting the shame and pain out of my body. Speaking our guilt and shame out loud is so incredibly healing.

When we give our pain and shame a voice and permission to be seen, we allow it to flow out of our bodies. When we allow others to help us heal it, it means we're not alone in our journey. Sometimes we want to keep all our shame to ourselves so no one sees it, and that separates us from others. It keeps them at a distance. Shame is in direct opposition to love. When shame is present, it's hard to fully feel love—for ourselves and for others. Shame competes for space. When we are full of shame, we can't be full of love. When we are full of love, we can't be full of shame. It's impossible. When we open our hearts and allow ourselves to be vulnerable, we know we're not alone and the healing journey becomes a little less dark.

Now I know that every time I don't speak up for myself, I let a small piece of myself go. I deny myself. I don't trust myself. And there's an underlying shame that comes with that, even if we don't realize it. The secondary layer of shame we can feel is the shame of not speaking up. And when we feel the shame of giving ourselves away and not speaking up, we learn not to trust ourselves. We learn we can't count on ourselves to stick up for ourselves. We don't have our own back. And when we don't have our own back, who does? I don't say this to mean you can only count on yourself, that you can never count on others, but to say you have to know and trust yourself first. That is where the depth and strength of our being lies. When we trust ourselves and know we can count on ourselves, life becomes so much easier. When we know we have our own back, it gives us the courage to be vulnerable with others.

A week later, my son wanted to talk about something really important.

"Hey, Mom, you have a minute?"

"Sure, what's up?"

"Well, I really want to thank you for our conversation the other day. I know it took guts. And I know it was hard for you. It really shifted a lot of things for me, Mom. So, um, yeah, you also inspired me to begin a hard conversation I need to have.

"I'm not happy in my marriage, Mom. In fact, I've been incredibly unhappy. But all this time, I've stayed because I thought it was the right thing to do. Now, I'm not so sure."

We chatted frequently over the next several days, talking through all his feelings about getting a divorce. And even though he knew it was going to be hard, he was ready. He had a safety net. He no longer felt alone and had the emotional support he needed to make this decision. He was willing to know his truth and not be afraid of it. He was willing to ebb and flow through the pain and make changes as needed. He had the courage to do the hard thing he thought he would never do. He thought he would be in the marriage forever and would just have to pretend to be happy. But after witnessing my brave authenticity and courage to stop pretending everything was okay, he realized he no longer needed to pretend anymore either. He had no idea how his wife would react. He just knew this was his next step forward and that having a hard conversation was okay.

I am constantly blown away by the profound effect we have on our children. They watch and observe everything we do. And how when we can claim our own wounding and the healing of it and claim our responsibility, it ripples out to everyone. We help others heal even when we're not aware of it. I realized in speaking up and sharing the shame I'd felt for years, not only did I heal my own wounds and perhaps help him start healing his but I also gave him an incredible gift. I showed him that by claiming and healing our shame and having the hard conversations, we can liberate ourselves. Because of his courage and willingness to no longer pretend, my son eventually got a divorce and started a new life. I am so proud of his willingness to step into the uncomfortable unknown and speak up for what he knew to be true for himself.

When we release our shame, we release ourselves. Shame is like shackles. It has an incredible hold on us. When we allow it to remain dormant, it stays locked in tight with no key. When we become aware of our shame and are willing to be curious about it and feel it, we unlock our pain and can release ourselves from those shackles. This is the key to unlocking the depth of us. This releases us from addictions, anxiety, self-doubt and criticism, and feelings of unworthiness. We stop projecting all this outward because we've released it from within. This is our ultimate healing.

Doing this work is not easy. It asks us to be brave and courageous. Feeling our pain takes energy and commitment. It requires us to allow the unfolding to happen without judgment. It calls us to be gentle and nurturing with ourselves. And often, when we think we've done an enormous amount of releasing and healed a major wound, another one is close behind it, ready to make its way out. And that's perfect. We might be exhausted from the work we've just done, but this is where we get to trust the process, surrender to the journey, and know it's all perfect. It wouldn't be showing up if we weren't ready.

Today I'm still asking for courage to do hard things and speak up so I can show up for myself and everyone around me. This deep asking comes from a place of knowing I'm here to be of service to the world. I know it's my daily asking and desire to be of service that allows me to continually move forward, step by step, no matter how hard or easy it is.

As I found my voice, things began to shift.

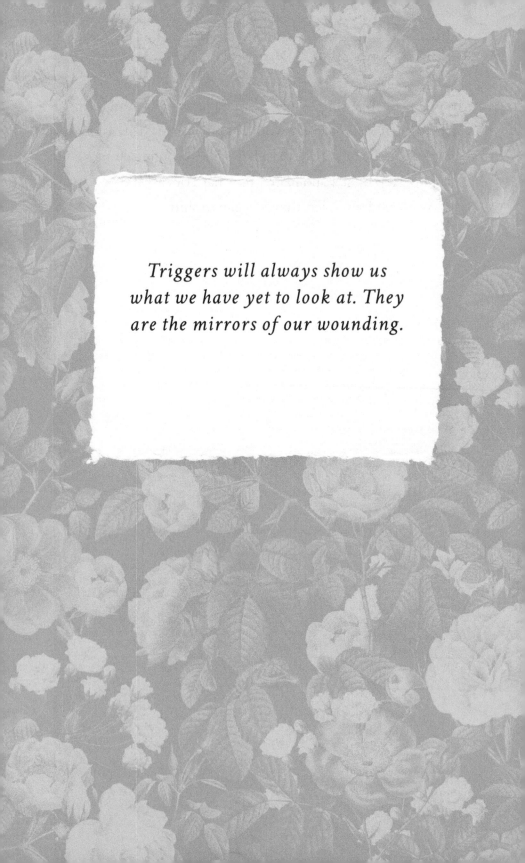

Triggers will always show us what we have yet to look at. They are the mirrors of our wounding.

9

DANCING

My husband and I have tried to divorce each other three times. We've hired lawyers. We've paid them lots of money. We've yelled and screamed and each played the victim. And after each unsuccessful attempt, we've landed back at the same place. We love each other deeply and are committed to making this work. I've known since the day we walked down the aisle that my marriage is supposed to be deep and meaningful. I didn't know what that looked like. I didn't have a particular example to look at. Maybe I thought I was supposed to forge my own path. All I knew was that what I was creating was going to be beyond what I knew marriage to be.

Ten years into our marriage, we started seeing individual therapists who would encourage us to speak up for ourselves, take care of ourselves, and show us where we were falling short of this. I was struggling to communicate properly. I would inevitably take the back seat. I would try to use manipulation to get my way rather than just saying what I needed. My husband used passive-aggressive communication and anger to get what he wanted. And even though I knew what he was doing, I didn't speak up.

Our therapists pointed out these individual unhealthy habits and behaviors, and then they'd show us how they were manifesting in and negatively impacting our relationship. They showed us how to shift our patterns. We each learned how to have ground rules and proper communication between us, especially when we argued. We learned that we could set boundaries, like no name calling, no walking away during an argument, no eye rolling, no scoffing at the other person, no demeaning language, no putting each other down in front of others. We brought these boundaries into our marriage and implemented them. And they would work for a while. Life would be good. So, we'd stop seeing our therapists.

Then the bubblings would start again. Another layer of our triggers would come to the surface. We'd start the argument cycle once again. I'd go back to therapy and learn new skills. I'm sort of masochistic when it comes to uncovering my wounds and healing them so I can move forward. I'm always curious as to what's hiding in my shadows. Not all of us want to routinely dive in and feel our pain in that way. It's not for everyone.

George doesn't share my enthusiasm in this area. He would search out a therapist when he thought it was necessary for him. He was more laid back with his approach. He would tell me he'd worked on his stuff, that he was using the tools he'd learned, and he didn't want to do any more for the time being. I wanted to teach him all that I'd learned, and he would often fight against that. He didn't want to engage with what I had to say. He was fine with where he was.

I thought that because I continued doing the work, he should be too, right along with me. I thought the only way to do the journey was to do it together. How was I supposed to love him if I continued growing and changing? How was this relationship supposed to work properly if I was always doing more work? I was stuck in my belief that it had to look a certain way, that our journey had to look the same, that we both had to evolve together. What I hadn't yet realized is that we all do this journey in our own perfect time and that our time doesn't always coincide with others' timelines or preferences.

These patterns of getting triggered, nearly getting a divorce, making up, and triggering each other again would go on for years despite our individual therapy work. Just because we were uncovering old wounds and healing old behaviors didn't mean there weren't many left to be healed. Neither of us realized that it would take us years for each of us to uncover all our woundings.

George and I were still on our individual journeys, finding out what we really needed and healing our own wounds. We struggled to move forward as a couple. We weren't really aware of the depth of our own woundings and all the triggers that were constantly rising to the surface. We would ping pong from trigger to trigger. We were trying to figure out who we were individually and in our relationship. We were clueless as to who our true selves were since they were so deeply buried. And even though George was doing his work and I was in therapy, we were still far from finding ourselves.

What I started to realize is that relationships are the path by which we find ourselves.

Triggers will always show us what we have yet to look at. They are the mirrors of our wounding. The triggers will only be there if there's a wound; otherwise, it would flow right off our back and would be a non-issue. Our relationships, every one of them, are here not only to provide us with love, support, and friendships but also for us to heal our triggers and wounds. Our relationships show us how far we've come, and they show us what's still ready to be released. It's the proverbial onion always being peeled back.

Each time we'd land at an impasse in our communication, we would try to get divorced. We hadn't quite yet learned how to own our triggers and find what was underneath. We needed to be more honest with ourselves and each other. We hadn't learned how to be truly vulnerable with each other by being able to identify and say what we were feeling. We still had our guards up.

Throughout the years of seeing our therapists, no one suggested we had unhealed trauma. I'm sure they knew it; they just didn't say it. Core wounding never came up for either of us. Our therapists were good, and the work we did kept us moving forward, yet neither of us was aware of the underlying trauma fueling all of this drama. When we think of childhood trauma, we automatically think of abuse. But it's not limited to this. Childhood trauma can also be from a sense of rejection or abandonment, whether from someone dying, leaving, or simply not being around, which as an adult, leads to trust issues.

For example, I didn't know how to trust men. The kinds of relationships I had with men didn't foster any sort of trust. Life taught me men were here to tell me what to do, lay down the law, punish me if I did something wrong, tell me what was best for me, and take advantage of me. They used coercion to get what they wanted. They bullied me. They put me in a state of fear, which can be a powerful motivator in how we make choices. Being afraid keeps us in a stagnant, passive space. I didn't think I was worthy enough to speak up for myself, to claim what I needed, to speak what was true for me, to go against the grain. With the woundings and false beliefs that life taught me, I willingly played into all the fear.

Let me get really clear on how fear controls. It might be fear of being neglected by a parent, in which case we alter our behavior in an attempt to not be left behind. We might be afraid of violence, verbal abuse, or being bullied, and we alter our behavior to avoid getting hurt. Maybe we grew up with an alcoholic parent and we learned to change all the ways we behaved in order to avoid their outbursts as best we could. As a child, all we want is love and acceptance from our parents or caregivers. We usually do whatever it takes to get that. We're desperate for love. Even if this love is narcissistic, abusive, part-time, or controlling. As we become adults, unless they are consciously addressed, all these unhealed issues remain in our psyche, untouched and unseen.

As humans, we keep our hearts closed because being vulnerable means being seen. Being seen can mean others see our faults and our shame. Keeping our hearts closed means we don't have to open up to others and let them see the real us, and *we* don't have to see the real us. Maybe we don't even know who that is. For some of us, being vulnerable and seen has brought us shame and abandonment. Maybe being vulnerable has taken away a source of love. And with that, we've learned it's a lot safer to just keep the heart under control. Our open heart can be a super scary place to allow someone to access.

Even though I was doing a lot of work on myself, my relationships weren't healthy, including the one with myself. My heart still wasn't fully open. I was guarding myself. I was scared to really be seen. I presented only the person that I wanted others to see. I thought I wasn't good enough just as I was, so I constantly looked to others to tell me what to do, to speak up for me, to be my advocate. I was always waiting for someone else to swoop in and save me from myself because the self I was presenting wasn't all that great. Everything in my life had taught me to look outward for who I was and to rely on others to guide my life. I had no idea it was my prerogative to speak up unapologetically for what I wanted and take control of my life. I was lost. I didn't know what a healthy relationship looked like—with myself, a man, or anyone else for that matter.

Unless we are deeply aware of ourselves and how we operate, we get into relationships that are familiar to us, that feel comfortable, that are what we're used to. It doesn't matter if the comfort level is abusive or narcissistic or super supportive and loving; it's what our psyche knows and what we're drawn to. If what we're used to is a loving, supportive, non-judgmental, and open environment, then that's what our psyche seeks out. Anything else will feel wrong to us. The energy will be off. We might not be able to identify it; we'll just know something is off. Conversely, if we're used to giving up ourselves to please others and making sure everyone around us is happy, even if it's at our own expense, then our psyche seeks this out. We truly don't think we're worth more than that. It's where our comfort lies.

And as adults, we will continue this cycle in relationships until we realize we're in this pattern. We'll be dumbfounded as to why all our relationships look the same and why we keep attracting the same partner. It's because we haven't yet identified these conditioned beliefs and behaviors. When we finally identify the roles we've been committed to playing, we can start seeing all the ways they've been alive in our lives.

Throughout my years and years of therapy, I've realized the role I played in my marriage and in all my relationships was because of my unhealed wounds. Growing up, I watched my parents argue. I don't blame them. As I see it now, they were battling with their own unhealed trauma and wounding. Even though my parents are both good people in their own right,

I watched them constantly struggle with who they were, who they thought they were supposed to be, and who they actually wanted to be.

At the time my parents grew up, the roles of the man and the woman were deeply entrenched in my parents and in society. They accepted these roles as the truth, yet continued to struggle, knowing there must be something else. I watched my mom seek independence and control as a way of fighting against the old dogma that men were in charge. At other times, I saw her want to acquiesce to my father even though she was living in an evolving culture that told her to be strong and not follow a man.

My dad learned that the man was always at work, paying for the needs of the family and being the provider rather than interacting with the family. Because he followed this path, he was rarely home. He and I didn't have much of a relationship when I was growing up. As a young girl, I wanted time from my dad. I wanted him to validate me. I wanted him to tell me that I was perfect just as I was. He wasn't home and I didn't get it.

When I got married, I looked for the same thing in my husband. I craved love, attention, and validation from a man, and I thought George would give it to me. I didn't know that, at the time, he didn't have any of this to give me. He was still stuck in his own unhealed trauma. His life filters taught him he needed to be in charge, take command of what was going to happen, have the last say, and use fear as a control mechanism. He was our financial provider and he was in the military, which meant he was rarely home. This was the exact pattern I was familiar with. I know you've heard "you marry your mother" or "you marry your father." I did exactly that. I married my father and became my mother.

My husband fit the bill of being the "man of the house." And I ended up behaving just like my mom. I acted and reacted the same way I'd watched her behave. I naturally played the part of the submissive. But since I was also constantly trying to control my environment, I learned how to covertly be the controller and not let George be in his masculine energy. I would tell him what to do, try to control his schedule, and make him feel guilty if he wasn't doing what I thought he should be doing. Guilt is a strong controller. And I was subconsciously creating drama just like my parents had.

My husband also grew up with drama and chaos in his family. As children, we both tried hard to be quiet to avoid drama that would get us in trouble. Until we realized we desperately wanted to be seen. As adults, we were always trying to be seen, however that looked. And as married adults, we were the drama queen and king of our household. We had no idea how our upbringing affected our daily lives. Chaos was deeply ingrained in our being. It was familiar, even if it wasn't always comfortable.

During a Mastermind group I participated in several years ago, one of the ladies suggested I was addicted to drama. I'd never heard of such a thing. Initially, I thought she was crazy. She insisted that some of us perpetuate drama in our lives because it's what we've known growing up. We cause situations to unfold with lots of struggle because it fuels our behavior patterns. I sat with this and realized it was true. When there isn't drama going on, we'll find ways to make it happen. Creating drama brings attention and excitement: we get the spotlight and a hit of endorphins. It's what some of us think love looks like. I began doing research on drama addiction and realized it's our brains' response to early childhood trauma. Drama addiction brings us a sense of satisfaction and control, both of which were missing in my life.

I was also shown growing up that being feminine directly means being a mother. I've mistakenly taken this to mean we must become the mother of our husbands, who then play the role of obedient child. We're supposed to tell them what to do, scold them when they're out of line, and judge and shame them when we feel it's appropriate. I would nag and insist I knew best. I subconsciously believed that I was the right one and George was the wrong one.

When we nag our partner, both of our energies shrink simultaneously. Mine shrank because I was nagging and trying to be in control, and his shrank because he was being nagged and not allowed to be himself. Trying to be in control of another human being is out of alignment with our soul. It's so confusing and overpowering to both the masculine and the feminine when the feminine tries to be in charge of everything.

Women's Lib was big when I was growing up. It was the "I am woman, hear me roar!" revolution. This was the woman who exclaimed she didn't need a man to survive in the world. It was the woman trying to break out of the mold the only way she knew how. A woman who could raise the kids, bring home the bacon, and fry it up in a pan. She was doing life all by herself and didn't need a man to make her better or bring home the bacon. She was completely able to operate on her own.

On the one hand, I thought this was great. Because of my wounding and misdirection from men, I also wanted to portray the chest-beating woman who was self-sustaining and independent. Simultaneously, I wanted a healthy relationship with a man, but I didn't know what that looked like. What I witnessed at home and from the generations of women before me showed me something different, and society was telling me that I really didn't need one anyway. What in the world was a woman supposed to be? I was completely clueless.

The man's role has equally been misunderstood. The men around me thought they were in control, had to use force and manipulation to get things done, insisted it be done their way, had to be the "tough guy," and couldn't show their feelings.

In recent decades we've had a swing to the opposite end of the pendulum, and the prevailing ideology developed that men being in their masculine is wrong or bad, that they need to be softer like a woman. Which then led them to fear of being a man. This was most likely in reaction to the movement of Women's Lib. Men lost their place in society. They confusingly stepped back from their place of leading and let women be more masculine. Just as I was doing in my marriage, women and society have been emasculating men.

Men have learned it's not safe to show up in their balanced masculine power. In saying this, let's not forget it is easy to abuse strength and power to get what we want, which we've interpreted as "the patriarchal energy." This energy hasn't always felt safe. Historically, men have led with force and control, only because, I believe, they found women's intuition and self-guided confidence to be threatening, thus history unfolded for them to forcefully be in charge. Few role models exist to show what a balanced, healthy, masculine man looks like. Men are just as confused about who they're supposed to be as women are.

The current crumbling of our world and its systems is the crumbling of the old patriarchal ways, of the old masculine ways of pushing and forcing rather than surrendering and allowing. The old ways of manipulation and deception are no longer needed. Rather, we need clear communication and transparency. The Divine Masculine is the warrior, here to fight the sacred fight; he is full of focused action, self-responsibility, and equality. He possesses self-restraint and self-awareness. The Divine Feminine is here to guide us back to ourselves, to knowing ourselves at our deepest level. She is the one who waits and allows all to unfold at the perfect pace. Now is the time we are all waking up to who we truly are.

Together, these distorted identities of male and female have led us to imbalanced roles today. It's not that men can't be soft and nurturing and women can't be strong and powerful. We all have both masculine and feminine energies within us;

it's the yin and the yang. One energy is the giver and one is the receiver. One is passive and one is active, and this shows up within all of us depending on the moment. It's a perfect balance of energy, yet we've forgotten the dance of the two. We forgot they can live together simultaneously in perfection within ourselves and within our relationships. The dance is knowing what energy serves best in any given moment. When we find ourselves in a situation that calls for nurturing, we can be that. When we find ourselves in a moment that needs our leadership and take-chargeness, we can be that too. And if we need to take charge and also be nurturing, we can do that.

We have the ability to call on these energies as we need them. We don't have to be in a male body to have predominantly masculine energy. Nor do we have to be in a female body to have predominantly feminine energy. Our roles aren't predicated on the body we are in. We all possess the perfect balance of the Divine Masculine and the Divine Feminine. Are we allowing this balance to flow through us and flow through our relationships?

I've learned to recognize when I'm balanced—I am creative, allowing, and receiving in my feminine, and I'm still clear and precise in my masculine. For George to provide for me, I first have to know what it is I want and be specific with it. I need to express my needs to him and trust that he will bring it to me. When I have been clear in my needs, he can provide. Then I get to sit back and allow his gifts and service to flow to me.

As the feminine, we naturally want to allow the masculine to lead. However, for him to lead, we have to know we can fully trust him. We have to know that, when needed, he will take charge in a mindful and active way and that his first thought is to take care of us. He has to be trustworthy and safe, and we have to know he will fully be present to our needs. The Divine Masculine is grounded, responsible, accountable, logical, and trustworthy. He is connected to the warrior strength. He is here to be a provider, to take care of us while owning his faults and flaws, being self-responsible, knowing himself to the core, and living from the place of his own divine strength. It's not patriarchal, structural, or hierarchical; it's the natural flow. This is part of the dance of creation. We cannot do this alone.

Understanding the flow of balanced masculine and feminine energy helped me see the trajectory of my own evolving dance in our relationship along my healing journey. In the past, I was covert in my needs. I didn't know how to articulate what I needed. I didn't know how to be fully present with him and reveal my feelings. I didn't allow myself to be vulnerable. I didn't feel safe within myself, and I didn't feel safe being vulnerable with him. After years of personal and relational practice, we have cultivated a relationship that looks completely different from where we started.

Now I believe the male and female are here to dance equally together. We each need the other to complete our purpose on this planet. We are both equal on this journey of awakening. We both need each other to unfold into our individual wholeness.

The masculine needs the feminine to be in the total truth of who she is. And, equally, the feminine needs the masculine to be in the total truth of who he is. Being in the truth of who we are requires us to heal our old wounds so we can be emotionally responsible for ourselves in the world. Healing our old wounds means having the courage to recognize where we've been numb and find the core of our own pain, feel it, and release it from our body. This allows us to hold more love.

We are here to awaken the Divine Feminine. And in order to do this, we require the Divine Masculine to be right with us. It's the only way it works. It's time to shift the perception of who we are as a whole. We both must have enough self-awareness to understand that the dance even exists in the first place and that each of these energies needs the other to thrive, to grow and develop as a human. The Divine Feminine is rising to bring back the balance. There is a massive healing that has to happen for Her to rise again, and that is what's happening right now on the planet.

As our world moves faster and faster, it's so easy to get lost in the constant pace of our lives, constantly doing, pushing, forcing, and striving. But as we move into this part of our history, the Divine Feminine is here to guide us on our path. We are moving forward with Her. She is showing us the way to get in alignment with who we are. She's showing us an easier way to live. Previously we had muted ourselves because we were afraid to say too much, or anything at all, lest we offend the masculine. This was submission out of fear. The opposite of this is submission out of love. And when we submit out of love, the journey is one of growth and joy and happiness. The journey is one to be taken together, yet it's a journey of the self before it's a journey combined.

Today I know exactly what a powerful woman looks like. And actually, this powerful woman is ever-evolving. She is a woman who knows the depths of her soul. She's gone deep within her shadows and held herself through all the pain she's buried. She's asked for help when she needs it. She doesn't avoid a healing experience because it might be uncomfortable. She knows it's all for her highest good. She's not afraid to feel her feelings and the truth, even when they are scary. She sees them and allows them to be with her. She allows herself to be vulnerable. She will step into her triggers so she can heal her wounds and be of greater service to those around her. She will feel all her discomfort to find the core of her pain. And then she will heal it. She will sit with her trusted sisters and allow their love and wisdom to catapult her forward into whatever life brings her.

If she is in a relationship, she knows the deep desire to emotionally climb onto her partner's lap and unfold the depths of herself, and feel safe. A powerful woman knows her partner can hold her full range without judgment. She knows her partner can hold everything when she needs to let go and fall apart. Because through this falling apart, she can be more of who she came here to be. She lets him into her most vulnerable places, the places that she thinks no one knows.

It's her stopping and being so he can do. It's in allowing him to help her, to take charge when needed, to allow his strong presence in her life to take place. It's allowing him to lead again. And she knows her partner can hold the greatness that is her.

And here's the thing about a strong awakened woman. She is unstoppable. She is an untethered force of nature. She knows her truth, and she's not afraid of it. She speaks with love and honesty. She has experienced the depth of herself and knows what she is capable of. She is wisdom. She is compassion. She is peace. And this woman is soft. She is gentle. She is patient. She is creative and nurturing. She is pure love. And she is submissive. She is submissive to creation. She is submissive to the flow of life. She is submissive to her partner, but only when he is in his greatest Divine Masculine. She is the creation of life itself. She exudes sensuality and all-encompassing earth energy. She is constantly changing. She ebbs and flows as she needs to. She focuses inward on herself rather than outward on the world. She is the Divine Feminine. And within us all lives the Divine Feminine waiting to be claimed, seen, and expressed.

I've been seeking my whole life for what and who I am here to be. For me, being the truth of me in the world means I'm here to awaken the Divine Feminine. For me to be that in the world means I need to heal my old wounds. It also means I need my counterpart of the Divine Masculine to be doing his work on himself and taking emotional responsibility for how he shows up with me and the rest of the world. When we do this dance together, I get to be fully me in the world.

We are unable to unconditionally love others until we are able to unconditionally love ourselves.

10

LOVING

Sitting on the leg machine at the gym, I was listening to a YouTube video of a woman who is a psychic medium and reads energies. She said, "This week's energy is all about revealing hidden secrets. They're gonna come out, so get ready, and it will be about one of two things: either work relationships or romantic relationships." I knew immediately she was talking to me and that it was the romantic piece. She was talking about my husband. Since she was talking about revealing hidden secrets. I sat for a second, wondering what this was. I wondered what he was hiding from me. As I sat, I got an intuitive hit he'd had an affair. It was the first time this had crossed my mind in the nearly 30 years of our marriage. I sat in silence on the machine and stared into space.

I questioned my thoughts. *Is this true?* I checked my intuition, and I was getting a *yes*. At this point in my life, I'd done enough work on myself and practiced enough to know

I could trust my intuition and what a *yes* feels like in my body. But I was in disbelief. I was having a hard time wrapping my head around it. This information was huge, and it scared me. *What did this mean for our marriage? Were there more secrets? Was our marriage over? Where did this knowing come from? And why now?* I finished my workout and walked out to my car. Everything around me was a blur as if I was moving and everything else was standing still. I drove home with all this in my mind.

I knew I needed to get home and sit with it. I cleared my calendar for the rest of the day and let this information be in my body. Everything internally told me an affair had happened, but I didn't have the verification from him yet. The Universe had put all the intuitive information neatly in my lap in a matter of hours. So now what? I sat outside in the sun, listened to the birds, and felt into everything I was feeling. I was numb and utterly confused. *When did this happen? Where was I when this was going on? Why did this happen?* I sat for hours observing my thoughts and feelings. I noticed I wasn't mad, which was really curious to me. I didn't feel resentful. Nothing in me wanted to make him the bad person. I was more curious than anything.

After sitting for hours, I realized he would be home from work soon. I was nervous. I was nervous because I knew the only way forward for me was to ask him if this was true. There was no going back. My mind was telling me this could go a million different ways. He could deny all of it, which would lead me to question my intuition severely. He could say yes and tell me he loved someone else. He could tell me it was still going on. He could tell me it had been happening with different women since we got married. My soul told me, even with all these questions, the way forward was through conversation. And that I was strong enough and wise enough to walk through this.

As I waited for him, I thought I'd better have all kinds of talking points ready, but my intuition kept telling me to be in this, moment by moment, second by second, to ask a question then listen to his answer. Then ask another question and listen to his answer. So I did. He came home and walked outside to sit with me on the back deck. We chatted for a few minutes about his day and a couple things that were happening at work. He stood up to go inside when I asked if we could chat for a minute. As he said yes and started to sit down, I watched him turn his chair more to face me. I took in a breath and let it out, "Have you had affairs in our marriage?"

His face flushed. He looked away. His body shifted. He covered his mouth with his hand and took a deep breath. Time stood still in that split second between my asking and his telling. In the silence, I knew his answer. My intuition was confirmed.

"Yes," he said.

My stomach turned. My reality changed in an instant. What I believed to be true over all these years wasn't. It hadn't been just the two of us in this marriage. There had been others. I had no idea what else he was going to tell me. Were we still going to be married after this conversation?

As I sat there, I checked in with myself. I had no anger,

no jealousy, just questions. I was in the moment with him and this information. I watched him sit with his emotions, with his shame, his regret, his fear. I wondered what question to ask next. He looked at me.

"When?" I asked.

He told me when it happened.

"Why?" I asked.

He reminded me what was going on at this time in his life, not that it was an excuse, but to provide the bigger picture of why. He began taking responsibility for his actions. He said it was one of the darkest times of his life. He'd been spiraling inward and didn't know how to get out. He was constantly trying to escape his reality, and this was one of the ways. He told me the guilt he's carried around has been enormous. He was getting emotional and said he thought he would never be able to let this out and was going to have to take this with him to his grave. He held his face in his hand for a long time.

I was in awe and curiosity of my calmness and stillness. Wasn't I supposed to be mad or yelling right now? Wasn't I supposed to be creating some sort of argument? Where was the drama? He said this had nothing to do with me, that it wasn't because I did or didn't do something. It wasn't because he didn't love me; it was purely because he was trying to escape his reality.

I felt his sincerity. I felt his truth and this was it. This wasn't about me. It was his journey, his pain. Not mine. I didn't need to speak or add anything or make him feel better or worse. I realized none of this triggered me. I didn't feel like a victim. I saw his pain and felt compassion. I didn't feel like I needed him to save me from myself. And I didn't feel I needed to save him from himself. He was strong enough to do this on his own. What I needed in that moment was to be quiet, listen, and be honest with myself. And that's exactly what I was doing. I realized we were two separate human beings having two separate experiences of life, and, in this moment, his experience had nothing to do with me. It was all his. To have had any other response than this would have been me trying to project something that wasn't there.

In that moment, I realized this was the result of my work to release shame. I was able to hold all this information with him and have no reaction. I didn't need to react. What I did do was hold a space of unconditional love, first for myself. My first thoughts of concern as we sat together were for me. I asked myself how I was feeling. I thought about what I needed in that moment. I knew I was strong enough to work my way through this. And I knew I trusted myself to take care of me. Then, I was able to hold this space of unconditional love for him so he could release his shame and guilt. I had no reaction because there was nothing for me to draw on. I didn't have deep wounding that still needed to be healed. I had seen my dark parts and learned to love them.

That's not to say that I'm done doing internal work. What I'm saying is that the immense amount of work I *have* done has cleaned out the insides. For us to have a reaction to someone else's behavior means we are still holding onto our own guilt and shame that's in some way connected. We still have wounds and triggers that we haven't loved. When we don't feel the love and acceptance of ourselves, when we're constantly silently judging ourselves, we're also doing all of this to others. We can't give what we truly don't have. When we don't feel deep acceptance for ourselves, we can't give it to others. We'll always find a way to judge and be divisive. We can pretend we love and don't judge others, but pretending only gets us so far.

Holding onto our shame and pain is what gives us fuel to fire anger and shame right back at someone else. I had nothing. I had no deep shame waiting to rear its ugly head, no guilt hidden in the dark corners. There were no triggers for me anywhere in this story to attach to. He'd said it happened years ago. He wasn't in love with anyone else. He did it purely because he was trying to escape. I was able to sit and listen to him tell me all of this, and I had no judgment.

As I have continued through my journey of healing my shame and my guilt and the things I've deemed unworthy, I've released so much of my own judgment and criticism toward others. I don't need it anymore to deflect my own pain. It's when we don't examine our own dark corners that we judge others and become so critical. For us to be us, we have to allow them to be them without judgment or criticism. When we let go of all the baggage we've held onto, we let go of wanting to make others wrong or bad. And when we can do this, we make room for love to live inside us.

We are unable to unconditionally love others until we are able to unconditionally love ourselves. For so long, I was looking outside for love because I hadn't yet learned to love myself. A million people on the planet could have told me they loved me, and I wouldn't have felt it. It took me getting inside and feeling everything that, up until that point, wasn't safe to feel. I started my own healing by loving all the parts of me I thought were unlovable. I started peeling back all the layers until I got to the small little flame that was inside me. Until I could love the smallest part of me that I deemed unloveable, nothing or no one else could be fully loved. We all think we're unlovable to some degree until we go to our deepest, darkest place and love and accept what is there. Now that I have found that core piece, I know I am fully loveable, first and foremost by me. I have never felt so comfortable in my body as I do now.

To date, this is the strongest I've felt in myself. I sat in my truth. I felt grounded in who I was. I knew in that moment I was able to handle something that could have completely rocked my world, and it didn't. That moment brought all the healing work that I'd done front and center and showed me the power I had within myself. I trusted myself to take care of me first. I knew I could sit with this kind of information and remain completely in love with him.

The dance that unfolded between us only happened because I allowed myself to fully be me. It was the truest sense of me without old shame, guilt, or old beliefs. The vibration of my truth allowed him to hold the vibration of his truth.

And the vibration of truth he held allowed me to continue to hold mine. The vibration of complete truth is love. In those moments, I was able to hold truth and love for myself and for him, which allowed him to match me. And his matching brought our energy together. This is a constant practice for me. I'd love to say that once I reach this place I can remain in this frequency, but I can't. I'm human. It's a state of flow that I come in and out of because I'm here to learn, feel, and experience. Life happens every day. And I know I have the tools to handle it.

As I continued in this place of acknowledging my strength and releasing my shame, another life event began to unfold for us. He had recently been let go from his high-paying job, almost without warning. A big life transition like losing a job or choosing to stop working happens because something in our lives is ready to shift. I was primed to help him through this process. I was like a giddy kid in class with ants in her pants, her arm raised, wrist wiggling, just waiting to be asked to answer the question.

But he didn't ask. He didn't ask for my help at all. *Okay. I'll give him this first week to just process everything, then I'll jump in with him and show him how it's done.* He still didn't ask. *Doesn't he know this is what I do? Coach people? I help them dive into their shadows to find the lessons? Didn't he remember I had a very similar experience and now had great understanding to bring to the table? This is my jam. It's what I'm really good at! I can help you!* He didn't ask.

I observed his behavior for weeks. I watched his moods

shift and swing. I watched him be super productive one day and lay on the couch and watch *The Sopranos* the next. *What's going on in his head? Why isn't he asking me to help him with this process? Why isn't he asking me for intuitive guidance? 'Cause I'm really good at that too!* It was so hard for me to not interject and tell him the intuitive hits I'd been getting and what I was observing.

One particular day, it was a *Sopranos* day, and he lay on the couch and told me how lost he felt, that he didn't know what to do. He felt deflated, he wasn't sure what he was supposed to be doing with his life, and he could only sit behind the computer for so long job hunting. As he was talking, so much intuitive information was coming in. I had lots of things I could offer him. When he finished talking, he said rhetorically and specifically not to me, "Am I just supposed to be patient?" Immediately I heard, "Yes!" I didn't say anything. I asked him if I could give him feedback, and he rolled his eyes.

Now, let me give a little backstory on the eye roll. In the past, I've given him lots of advice and guidance without him asking for it. Sometimes he wants to hear it, and sometimes he doesn't, and usually I give it anyway. I just think everyone is like me and would benefit from all the insight I can offer. I get so excited to dive into this stuff and find out what's hiding and ready to be healed and loved. It didn't ever occur to me that he didn't want to hear it. Not everyone's like me.

So, when he rolled his eyes, I totally knew and respected where he was coming from. He thought I was going to once again give him an overwhelming amount of information that he may or may not be ready for. This time I wasn't. I felt like he needed his space to do his own thing. I told him I didn't have to say anything, that it was fine. I was neutral in this situation. He begrudgingly said yes, and the only thing I was guided to share with him in that moment was, "Be patient."

Beyond this, I stayed silent. I chose to hold space and remain quiet. I wasn't hounding him about getting a job; I wasn't anxious or worried about it. Everything in me told me this was completely on purpose.

Later that week, I sat in my office and thought about this experience, and I looked at my vision board. It's on the wall in front of my desk. Each month I pick several tarot, angel, or energy cards to guide me through the month. One of the cards I drew for this month was the Mother Mary Energy card from the *Magdalene Oracle* deck by Toni Carmine Salerno. I looked at the card and saw her divine nature, her outstretched arms, her loving expression, the light radiating behind her. She was so present with me every day this month, watching over me, guiding me, and sending me messages that are deeper than I can understand. Some days I would look at the card, feel so much love, and pass it on to my family. I would look at her and hear words like *patience, compassion*, and *understanding*. Each time I heard a message from her, I felt like my vibration was rising as if she was vibrationally guiding me through the month. She was showing me how to open my arms wide and love my husband more.

Mother Mary's energy is so unconditionally loving. She

was showing me how to unconditionally love him as he journeyed through this process. She was telling me to let go of the expectations and the outcome I thought was supposed to happen and just love. She was telling me to hold space in a new way. This is the gift from the Divine. As I continued to look at her image on this card, I grabbed the book that gives more explanation to each card in the deck.

It says:

"Dearest One: I ask you to surrender the fear and anxiety you hold for a loved one's wellbeing. Trust. All will turn out for the highest good of all concerned. This situation is simply part of your loved one's life experience and learning. A blessing eventually stems from this current event. Remember, at the heart of all creation, only love exists. Allow divine love to stir within your heart; feel it move the Earth and stars as the miracle of life forever unfolds. Have faith in the universal spirit of life and know that you and those dear to you are eternally protected. I shower your loved one with protective and healing light, so please do not worry."

It can't get any clearer than that! She was specifically guiding me on how to love bigger.

Throughout my life, my struggle has been to regain my voice, speak up, say what I need to say, and be heard. And now, the greatest way I can show up for him is to stay silent. The biggest gift I can give him right now as he does his work is to not talk at all. I know. It's kind of ironic that I've spent so much time and energy trying to get my voice back, and now silence is the best way to serve. I'm in awe of this realization, of the full circle of how it's shown up. Nothing needs to be said. I don't need to speak. This is how the Divine Feminine shows up. It's the ultimate form of surrender and trust for me. Mother Mary sits with me as I am still and quiet. I am in full trust and knowing that he is on his perfect journey. The gift of unconditional love means I don't need to change, fix, or teach him. My gift is what I'm doing right now in this peaceful space of trust and silence.

What I understood in my chosen silence was that he was doing his processing exactly how he wanted to do it, and it was perfect. The masculine processes differently than the feminine. They don't necessarily want to call all their friends, chit-chat, and cry about their deepest, innermost thoughts. They're not touchy-feely like we are. He didn't have to dive in like I do. Maybe he never will. Maybe that will never be his process. Maybe he'll never hear all the intuitive downloads I got while he was talking. It doesn't matter. I thought a process should look a certain way and that lying on the couch in the middle of the day watching *Sopranos* wasn't it. But it was. It was his way. He was showing up for himself perfectly for his own journey, even though I wanted it to look different. I was realizing that I had an attachment to how his journey looked.

He knows exactly what he's doing, even when he thinks he doesn't. My job is to give him the widest berth he needs to do his process. I'm overwhelmed with gratitude by providing space for the man who's provided for me for all these years of our marriage. He's provided me lesson after lesson of growth.

Now, I get to hold this space of providing for him; it just looks different. He's provided for me financially; he's given me the opportunity to live in amazing countries and experience different cultures. He's provided me time and space to start businesses.

Now, my providing is an energetic providing. I get to provide him with a safe, loving place to unwind and just be and to work out whatever is going on internally. I know he's learning his own lessons because he incarnated here to do that. Had he not had the upbringing and life experiences he had, he would not have presented himself to me the way he did and still does. He's doing his job exactly as he contracted to do it. He has done this over and over. He has shown up for me in this way throughout our entire marriage. And the best thing is, he doesn't have to plan it out or be purposeful about it. He does it by just being him.

He subconsciously got himself out of a job not only for the lessons it's teaching him but also for the lessons that it's teaching me. He's letting me find in myself how the Divine Feminine ultimately shows up in her surrender and trust. His soul, his Higher Self, chose part of this journey of losing his job for me so that I can surrender and learn this piece of my journey. I'm overwhelmed by how much it takes to be still and how much of a gift he's giving me by allowing me to be still. And he doesn't even know what all this is doing for me. He's shown up perfectly for me to learn all these lessons I needed to learn so I can be me in the world.

Several days later, as I sat in my office writing, he came in and sat on the couch. I was still in the middle of a thought and asked him to wait just a second. He leaned his head back and closed his eyes. As he did, I felt the energy that I usually feel when I'm getting ready to channel information. My energy shifts. The back of my neck gets tingly. The vibration in my ears is different. I was still looking at him as all this was happening and realizing his Higher Self was talking to me. Immediately I opened up another Word document (and myself to be a channel) and started allowing the information to come through me. I heard his voice speaking to me in my head. I began channeling his Higher Self.

We are dancing together. I'll get fired from my job so you can figure this next piece of our life out. I'll do this for you. I came here to help you bring the Divine Feminine into the planet. I came here to help you usher it in. It's what I do. It's what I've always done. My purpose has always been to help you, you just saw it differently until now. I have been here doing exactly what we agreed to, as have you. My greatest joy has been to help you bring this manifestation into the world. Unfold into me more. Let me hold you as you go out into the world, as you walk out on the stage. I'll hold you, and I'll be right here for you and with you. We do this dance together. We are one.

I was blown away, yet not at the same time. I wasn't surprised that he was speaking to me in this way. As the energy of the channel finished, he opened his eyes and looked at me. He had no idea what had transpired. I smiled and mentally gave thanks for what just happened.

Now, I know he's here on this earth doing his own work—he's working on his own karma and healing his old trauma—but he also just told me he's been here supporting me in my mission all along. But really, aren't we all? Aren't we all here showing up together exactly as we knew we would for this mission? For our personal and collective missions? We are! My mission is to feel and know the depths of pain, shame, guilt, silence, and abuse. I came here to learn how to love myself unconditionally. I came to learn how to love others unconditionally. I came here to bring back the balance of the Divine Feminine and the Divine Masculine. I came here to write this book. I came here to be a beacon of light and to remind you of your light.

It's an emotional thing for me to process that he came here in support of me and my mission. His Higher Self just told me his main mission on this planet has been to support me, to support the awakening of the Divine Feminine. While I knew he was supporting me, it never occurred to me that we were working toward the same goal. This piece of the bigger picture of our marriage has never even been on my radar. I knew he was a great teacher by just being him, but I never conceived that our marriage held this higher purpose. His channeled message for me was to let me know that we're on the same page—that we're doing this work in the world together, that what he and I have been doing up to this point is perfect.

In the dance of the masculine and feminine, I am the receiver and he perfectly provides ways for me to receive. He gives me moments that invite me to get clearer with myself. When I'm triggered, he shows me my blind spots. When he's done something that doesn't feel good to me, it affords me the opportunity to use my voice and speak up. Still, there are times when we have hiccups in our communication and I want to take the back seat and not put effort into speaking my truth. When he's having a moment of wanting to take charge or take control without getting my input, this provides me the opportunity to speak up. He's not doing it on purpose. There's nothing planned about it. It's the natural ebb and flow of life that allows him to provide me with plenty of opportunities to receive in this way. It's how the masculine shows up. He shows up perfectly as himself so I can do what I am here to do. And simultaneously I show up perfectly for him, to provide what he needs.

As I continued to write and reflect on the imperfect perfection in how we were showing up for each other, I saw the heart-shaped rock sitting on my desk given to me by my girlfriends from Austin. It reminded me of how far I've come. Before I moved, we had a going-away dinner. Each woman held the rock and infused it with something they loved about me. I breathed deeply each time my friends spoke to tell me what they loved and then passed it on to the next. I was so filled with this love. It was overwhelming. This was one of the first times I felt worthy, seen, and held in a space of pure unconditional love. This group of women was showing me what it looked like to show up with so much love for another human being. My body didn't know how to receive it at first. I was shaking, and it took a long time to fully integrate. That was the starting point to learning what this kind of love felt like. It was also the first time I allowed this kind of love to flow into my being.

Everyone shows up for us to come into a fuller, deeper acceptance of ourselves. And this requires seeing all of who we are and letting others see that too. For a long time, it wasn't safe for me to be seen and loved in that way. I can claim now that I am lovable. That used to feel so shameful to claim or say.

What if you could be loved for exactly who you are? That is unconditional love. It's the energy we all incarnated here with. The energy of love. Over time, we've denied ourselves this love because it didn't feel safe. It is time to let ourselves be seen and loved in this way.

Now that I know I am fully loveable, first and foremost by me, I can more confidently live out my purpose. Until now, this level of self-love has been elusive because I was looking for it outside myself. Now that I've done so much internal work and know myself at my core, I know I am the one who needed to love me. And I do. I have never felt so comfortable in my body, being who I am, and doing what I am here to do as I do right now. I can feel love. I can give love. I can receive love. I am love.

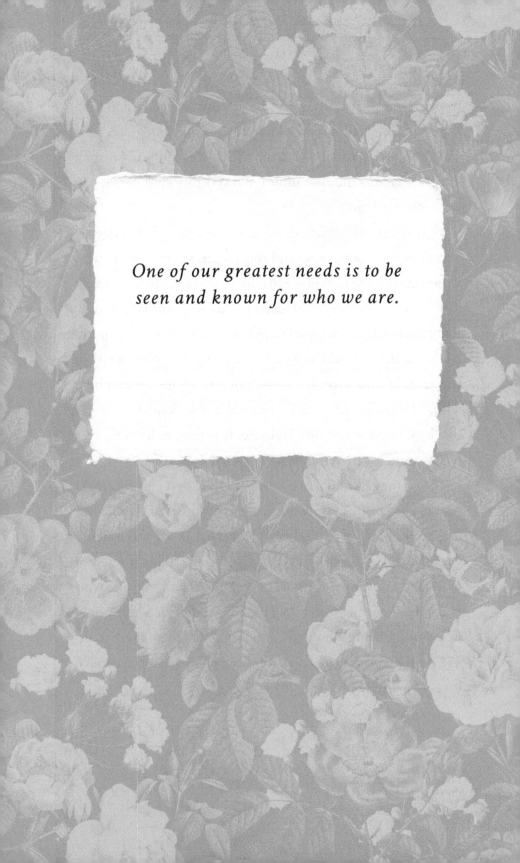

One of our greatest needs is to be seen and known for who we are.

11

SHINING

I'm at the gym, listening to music in my earbuds, extremely loud. My pussy reminds me she is ready. The music magnifies my feelings. I want sex. I want sex with him. I'm lifting weights but thinking about him and what I want to do when I get home. My pussy tingles when I think of him. I finish my workout and get in my car, still with my earbuds in. My music is still loud, my pussy getting wetter as I drive home.

It's slightly throbbing as I drive into the garage, turn off the car, close the garage door, and go inside. He's upstairs. I walk up the stairs as I'm taking off my clothes. My yoga pants are on the floor; my sports bra is on the couch. I open the door to his office. There is so much heat in my body. I'm ready. I take over. This moment is mine. It's all about me and what I want. I'm fully absorbed in myself. I'm ready for crazy, off-the-charts sex, so I make it all about me. I'm selfish. I make sure I'm the one being pleasured.

Still, he's enjoying himself immensely. His breathing is fast and loud. His hands grab me; they grab my head. The ebb and flow of energy between the two of us is electric. My sexuality is so present. Typically, I let him take charge or we go back and forth. But this time, I straddle him and take him with every part of my being. I want to own him, consume him, be in my fierceness. I want to encompass every part of his being. I am all of me with him. I unfold into my greatness. My pussy is on fire. My back arches. My eyes close. Electricity flows through me. I am on fire and can't stop. The release of myself with him comes to a crescendo. I explode into myself. I explode all over him. I am loud. I am primal. I am unapologetic in my expressions.

The greatness that is me encompasses the entire room we're in. I am perfection. My noises lessen, and I become silent. My body slows and stops. My eyes open, and in his eyes, I see a reflection of myself. He is in awe. He is thrilled that I allowed myself to go to that place. I went there—no shame, no guilt. I was at peace and fully surrendered to the pureness of the moment. He sees me. He sees all of me. He sees me in my nakedness, my sensuality, my power, my softness. He sees the truest, vulnerable part of me. That was fucking amazing!

Being seen requires being vulnerable. Vulnerability is how we know who we are. When we allow ourselves to open up and be seen by another, we find out who we are. By allowing others to see us fully, we access all parts of ourselves. That level of unbridled passion and freedom in our sexuality requires an enormous willingness to be seen. We have to trust ourselves. We have to know we are worthy and deserving of every single second of what's happening. We have to know the depths of who we are. And we have to trust our partner. We have to be willing to be vulnerable with ourselves first and foremost before we can be vulnerable and seen by others.

Being vulnerable with ourselves can be just as scary as being vulnerable with another. To see ourselves fully takes courage. It means we see and acknowledge all our flaws. It means we've done the work and looked within, into all the dark corners, shown a light into all the places where we hide ourselves. Having nothing left to hide or be ashamed of provides a path forward in our growth and trust in ourselves. We become curious about what's still there to be seen.

An experience like the one I just had with my husband doesn't unfold like that when we still have years of baggage hidden away. That moment happens when you're no longer hiding from yourself. Throughout my journey, sex came with so much shame and baggage. I was shamed for having sex. When I had sex and thought it was fun or wanted more, I felt wrong. The shame I've held onto has kept me from being the fullest and truest expression of myself.

Throughout my life, I've been told to quiet down, I was too loud, I was too much, and I brought this into the bedroom. I didn't allow myself to fully enjoy sex. I kept quiet and didn't make too much noise. I was subdued. I only allowed myself to be halfway committed to the pleasure. I didn't want to fully enjoy it because there was still something about it that felt shameful. I carried all this baggage with me into my relationship. I still held onto all these emotions and beliefs from what I'd been taught. On this cyclical journey of reclaiming who I truly am, I found my way back to exploring some major themes in my life. This is what the healing path offers—meeting these parts of ourselves in new ways.

According to my upbringing, sex was only for marriage, and even in marriage, no one told me the power and ecstasy that comes with letting yourself experience the erotic pleasure of it. I wasn't really supposed to enjoy sex that much. If I enjoyed it too much, what would he think of me? I didn't know how to let go and enjoy what was happening. When I did, I felt a hint of guilt, like I was doing something I wasn't supposed to be doing. Since I wasn't taught pleasure was good, for me, it meant it was bad, and too much pleasure translated into guilty, as in "guilty pleasure."

Sex is one of the most pleasurable acts we as humans get to have and enjoy. Sex is connection. Sex is primal and intimate. We are meant to use our voice in this act, to be loud and expressive or soft and quiet, as we desire. It's full of vulnerability and surrender. If we allow it, sex takes us to the core of our being. When we bring ourselves back into balance, this is what happens. When we have seen all our shame, healed our wounds, and are no longer afraid of what lingers in the dark, this incredible dance of sex is one of our gifts. To allow pleasure into our lives is a virtue of the Divine Feminine.

As humans, we're here to enjoy and experience the sensual pleasures of the earth. That includes receiving through all the senses—delicious foods, beautiful sights, intoxicating smells, and pleasurable touch. Most of us aren't taught to seek out pleasure, to look for fun, or to thoroughly enjoy ourselves. Or maybe we have been shown how to have fun, but only to a certain point. Some of us have been taught pleasure is tainted with a hint of guilt. We only know how to enjoy to a certain extent. A glass ceiling has capped our pleasure. We enjoy a dessert but work a week at the gym to get rid of it, or we restrict our eating to make up for it. We go on vacation but have to justify it with all the hard work we've done. Most of us are taught to live in scarcity and limitation. To only enjoy life to a certain extent, to not have too much fun, to not fully express ourselves.

Fully expressing ourselves is pleasurable. It's joyful. It's cathartic. Fully expressing ourselves also means allowing the pain to be front and center, not thinking we have to hide our tears or sadness. Experiencing the full range of our emotions is part of allowing ourselves to be fully here on this planet. Being able to fully access and express our range of emotions means we've tapped into the well of us. This is the Divine Feminine. This is the expression of her on earth. She is inherent in all of us. She is in each one of us. What's keeping us from letting her out? Our partner wants to see her. We want to see her. So why isn't she here? Where is she? Why is she hiding? What are we afraid of?

One of our greatest needs is to be seen and known for who we are. And for as hard as I worked on not being seen for the majority of my life, I was screaming at the top of my lungs TO be seen. But I only wanted you to see the parts of me I thought were lovable. I wanted to be seen for the gifts I brought into the world. I wanted to be seen for what I'm here to do. I wanted to tell everyone that I was here to help others, that I have gifts, that I could help you. I wanted you to see me, to know me.

I was trying to prove that I was worthy of being on this planet. My childhood wounding told me I wasn't worthy. Deep down, I didn't believe I was worthy of being here. I second-guessed my gifts. I doubted my abilities. As a little girl, I doubted I was here to help others heal. I stopped doing it. I've pulled the plug on my businesses, stopped my podcasts, and told myself that I didn't have enough to say to write an entire book. I didn't believe I was here to teach others how to open their minds and expand into new ways of thinking. I didn't think my normal life lent itself to any of that. My self-confidence was nil.

The first fifty-three years of my life have been a dichotomy of fiercely wanting to be seen yet not wanting to be seen at the same time. I've vacillated between beating my drum for what I'm here to do and remaining in the background, silent. I certainly didn't think I was here to speak up and share my truth or say, "This is who I am." I didn't actually want you to see all of me. I didn't want you to see my shame and guilt. I didn't want you to see the darker pieces of me.

With every secret and feeling of shame I've shared, I've

unleashed and let go of what's been hiding in the darkness. I've let go of decades of unhappiness, guilt, and anxiety. These feelings had taken up residence in my body. Releasing them, letting you see them through this book, and no longer feeling ashamed, releases these repressed emotions. They've left my body. My digestive issues and food allergies have healed themselves. They're no longer here. Doing this makes room for joy, for love.

When we commit to our self-healing and look at everything we've held onto our whole lives, do the work, and eventually let it all go, we free up this space for nothing other than love. Love is the purest vibration there is. Love fills the cells of our body. And when we hold this much love and light in our cells, it flows from us. We smile all the time. We laugh frequently. We feel the physical feelings of joy. And we can't help but love others.

Sometimes there can be shame in feeling so much joy and happiness. Others don't believe this is possible. People have suspicions when you're happy. They want to know *why* you're so happy. They want to take you down a notch. They want to dismantle it. They've never learned that this happiness also lies within them. They find it unbelievable and most likely scary. They cannot imagine that within themselves lies an unbelievable amount of love, joy, and happiness.

Growing up, there were times I'd feel a lot of love and happiness. And I'd want to share that with others. Sometimes it was welcomed; other times people didn't know what to do with my love and excitement and would tell me to calm down, reel it in, control myself. They would tell me I didn't need to get so excited, that I was too happy. I'd bring myself back in, restrain my joy. I didn't know at the time that my showing such an outpouring of enjoyment or excitement was triggering wounds in others. I internalized their actions to mean I was embarrassing them or I didn't know how to act appropriately.

I denied what was in my best interest. I denied my emotional and mental wellbeing, my purpose on the planet. I thought I wasn't on purpose, that I was living in the wrong family, that I was supposed to be somewhere else altogether. I began to doubt myself. I was born into a normal family. I have a normal family. How can I be normal and be in the greatness of a being like the Goddess Tara? Who am I to claim any of this? Who am I to be a beacon and shine so brightly, to be a beacon for your wounding?

Then I realized that for my entire life, everything I was doing and learning had been exactly on purpose. What I thought was wrong was perfectly right all along. I was on purpose the entire time. I was doing and learning what I needed to. Everything in my life has been perfectly orchestrated the way it was meant to be, to be of service to you now. At birth, I was indoctrinated into religion. I've experienced abuse and trauma. I've felt the depths of shame. I've pleased everyone around me and lost myself in the process. I've felt the acutely profound effects of all my emotions. I've been silenced, and I've stayed quiet. I've played small.

To do the work I'm here to do in the world means I have to be seen. I'm rewriting the rule I've subscribed to my whole life: that I wasn't supposed to outshine others. Only now, I realize I'm not outshining anyone. I'm just being me. I'm doing what I came here to do. I'm not competing with anyone or anything. Me being me allows you to be you.

As women, we've worked so hard at proving ourselves worthy of being here, of taking up space, and showing everyone around us that we can do it (whatever the IT was for us). We've worked our whole life at this. We've wanted to be understood for the incredible feminine energies that we are, so we made sure everyone knew we were here. Now, what if we are still doing exactly what we're here to do, but we don't have to prove anything to anyone?

When we're in the energy of having to scream to be heard or needing to beat a drum so someone sees us, there's part of us that actually doesn't believe we're worthy of being seen or heard in the first place. We don't believe in ourselves. We attach to a specific identity trying to find out who we are. When we create so much chaos and commotion just for others to see us, we have unhealed wounding within. This doesn't make us bad. It simply shows us we have some stuff to work on. We have deeper wounds that are ready to be healed. Otherwise, we wouldn't be proclaiming it.

Most of the time, we have to come full circle from not having a voice and not speaking up to over-talking and trying to make sure we're heard to finding and knowing we have a voice and that it's important. Finding our voice can mean we finally get to speak when it's our choice, when it's on our terms, when we choose to and want to, and when it's important to us. We have to know that what we're saying is important to us and it's important to who is hearing us. Having a voice can be subtle and can also mean we don't have to speak as much as we think we do.

What if the person that's here is already worthy of taking up space? What if the work we've done our entire lives is completely valid and valuable? What if we've been in service this whole time? There comes a point where we realize we're no longer trying to prove our existence with our voice.

I know now, after writing this book, that I have nothing left to prove to anyone—that the me that shows up today and every day is the perfect version of me. I no longer have to scream for you to see me. I don't have to beat my drum for you to hear me. I no longer need you to understand me or understand what I stand for. I no longer need to prove anything to you. I am more than good enough by showing up every day. I know that me being here is perfection. And I know what I'm here to do.

I've been liberated from so many of my fears. I'm still being liberated from myself, from my own old beliefs of what I can't do or what I'm "supposed" to do. But I'm not afraid of being bright and shiny anymore. I'm no longer afraid of what I signed up to do in this lifetime. I'm really clear on what it is I am here to do, and that is to awaken the Divine Feminine—that unstoppable, untethered force of nature who is constantly changing and knows what she's capable of because she has gone to the depths of her own soul and felt what's been hiding and is no longer afraid of her own shadow.

An internal shift within me has awakened me. I know I am her, Tara, The Divine Feminine. I know what I'm here to do, that I am here to emulate her greatness. And by emulating her greatness, I am reminding you of your greatness. I shine on you so you can see yourself. You see yourself in my reflection. I am a mirror for you. Whether you love me or you hate me, my light is doing exactly what it's supposed to be doing. It's shining on you. If you hate me, it's only because you have yet to allow the light to shine into your darkest corners. Wherever you are triggered by me are the places still asking to be healed. And if you love me, it's because you can see the parts of yourself that are doing exactly what you came here to do. You are already shining your light. You are already full of love and self-confidence. I am the expression of you as you are. I am the expression of all that is.

The more I shine and speak my truth, the clearer the way is for you to shine your light and speak your truth. It's back to the ripple. The more I remind you of what you already know you're here to do, the more you remember of yourself and the more you get to remind others of what they're here to do. The more of my own strength and wisdom I remember, the more I get to remind you of your own strength and wisdom, and the more you get to remind others of theirs.

I am here to remind you of your greatness. I hold your hands, and we become one. We are the greatness of the Universe. Together we are the Infinite. I know the bigness that is you. I see your Divinity. I see all of you. You are God and Goddess. You are everything. You've just forgotten.

I don't have any shame left in telling you my mission on this planet is to help you, that I'm here to help you however that looks. I am here to be a beacon. Whether we see each other in person and we get to exchange words, you attend a retreat, we get to do hands-on healing together, you read my books, or you hear me speak, I know that when we meet, you will receive exactly what you need to receive from me. I know with every fiber in my being that I—my energy, the being that I am on this planet—am here to help you shift. I am here to show you what this looks like for yourself. I'm here to show you how to uncover your wounds and heal them. I'm showing you that it is perfect to be in your most pleasured state. I am here to liberate you from yourself. I am here to free you from what no longer serves you.

When I share with you about the blissful state of having sex with my husband, I'm showing you there is no shame in having it, experiencing it, or talking about it. Trust that everything you see in me is perfect. If you see me and think I'm narcissistic, check in with yourself and see why you believe it's not safe to be fully you. If you see me and think I just came out of the blue and am claiming I'm here to shift a planet, ask yourself why you believe you can't do the same. If you see me and you see love, laughter, and joy, know that you are also shifting the vibration with your own love and laughter. You're also doing your job perfectly.

And by me being me, I'm already doing my job. I'm helping you shift. This is the perfection. And equally, when you are you, you are also doing your job. Even when you're in your grumpiest, saltiest, sour mood, you're still perfect, and you're showing up perfectly. You'll shift and let in light at exactly the right time. Maybe your saltiness is perfect for someone else who is learning how to navigate you. Maybe you're reflecting someone close to you, and they really need to see their own stuff. You are perfect right now. We are all doing our job together to collectively shift the planet. Trust in the timing of your life.

There is an incredible energy in writing these words. They come from the deepest knowing of my being. To put these on the paper means there's nothing of me left to hide. I'm no longer in the shadows. I know who I am to the fullest. Even as I write that last sentence, I know that the fullness of me will only grow. By claiming the fullness of who I am, it expands who I AM.

When we are finally able to claim the God-self within us, our energy is limitless. We can attract everything we are here to be, do, receive, and experience. There is nothing about this that is egoic. I thought that if I were to tell others I was here to help shift humanity, shift a consciousness, I would be thought of as a narcissist. I was so afraid of this label. It held so many meanings for me that I ran in the opposite direction. In order to serve others in the most impactful way, we have to put ourselves first. I have to think about myself and my wellbeing before I can think about others. There's the paradox. It's not negative to put oneself first.

When we get to the point that we know what we're here to do, we are claiming all that is us. It's claiming everything we are here to do and be. And when others try to tell us otherwise, it's only because they can't imagine they also came here for a purpose. We all want to know what our purpose is on this planet. And are we even serving that purpose at all? Before I go any further, let me just remind you that you are. You are exactly on purpose. You are exactly where you are intended to be right now; otherwise, you'd be somewhere else. You are right where you need to be to learn the lessons you wanted to learn and to serve the people you intended to serve. I know you're ready for this because you're here. You're here on this planet at this time. Right now. You're reading or listening to these words. You're ready!

There's an inner knowing telling us we're serving the exact purpose we came here to serve. Maybe you came here to be on stage and speak truths in the world. Maybe you came here to be a mother and raise amazing children, and in your heart, you know this is exactly your purpose. We are all here to be of service to each other in one way or another. The ultimate reclamation of our truth is claiming all that we are and all that we are here to be for ourselves and humanity.

SHINING

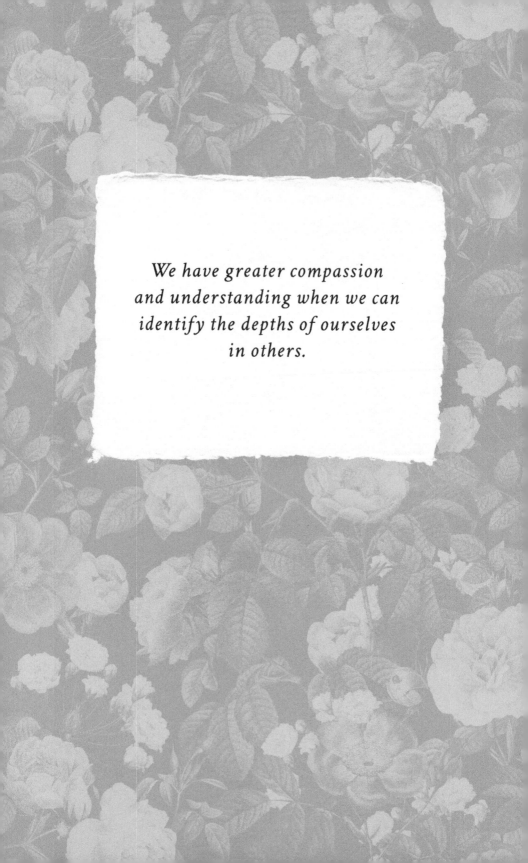

*We have greater compassion
and understanding when we can
identify the depths of ourselves
in others.*

12

EXPANDING

I'm sitting in my office having a Zoom call with my book doula. We're talking about the last chapter, how to wrap it up, how I express everything that's happened since I started writing this book, and how I'm going to wrap up the process of becoming me that's unfolded over the last year. We're talking about how I'm not even the same person I was when I started. We talk about all the internal work I've done, the old beliefs I've left behind, and the old patterns that I've shed. We talk about the wounding I've uncovered and how I've seen the depths of myself over the last year.

She reminds me to call on the Goddess Tara, my namesake, to be with me when I'm writing this chapter. As soon as she says these words, I have the image of Green Tara in my mind. Her energy envelops me. I can feel her with me in my office. I start to cry. I can feel her enormous energy all around me, in me. My body starts to shiver. I begin breathing deeply to allow the energy in my body. It's slightly overwhelming. I realize how big this energy is, and I feel like I almost can't hold it all, as if my small physical body isn't enough to hold all of her. My body starts shaking. I'm crying more. I'm overwhelmed by what's going on. I feel like my circuits might blow at any time.

Intuitively I know she and I are becoming one, even more so than before. The energy of me expands past my office walls. I feel as if I'm seven feet tall. I feel powerful, all-knowing, full of love and compassion. I know why I'm here. I feel my own confidence in what I've come here to do and accomplish. She is giving me all the information I'll need to do my job on this planet. She's downloading the codes, allowing them to penetrate my cells and all parts of my being. I keep breathing, allowing it all to be in me.

I realize this is more than I can do by myself, and I ask Amanda to help me ground all this energy. My eyes are still closed, and I hear her say, "I got it. I'm doing it." I feel it. I feel her strength as she holds space for what's happening. I feel her grounding us, and this allows me to keep going. I feel the information. I know exactly what Tara is doing. She's reminding me of what I came here to do, of why I'm here on this planet. It's to liberate others from their suffering and to hold compassion and wisdom for their journey. She's reminding me that my job is to hold this beautiful space while others realize their own truth. The energy of Green Tara and the downloads seem to go on for a while. I'm in a perfect state of bliss and just want to stay here. But my breathing starts to normalize. The shaking in my body slows down. I can feel the information starting to anchor and settle.

After several minutes of sitting with what just happened, I open my eyes. My doula is still with me. She sees me. She's held the perfect space with me for all that just transpired. Of course, she's with me right now; she's been the one with me through the entire process of writing this book. She has been a co-creative component in this process. She's the only person I would be doing this with right now. In my mind, I feel like I just gave birth. She tells me she feels like she just witnessed a birth.

We sit together in this, and she reminds me that at the beginning of this journey, almost a year ago, I wrote down that my office felt like a womb, and at the time, I wondered what I was birthing. I remember thinking I didn't feel the need to answer the question right away. I knew it would be answered when the time was right. Now I know. It's been a womb for everything that's happened over the last year and for this moment that just unfolded. I created my own sacred womb to birth Tara into the world. I know who I am. I am Tara. This information is grounded and solidified in me. Now I know what it feels like to embody her as a human and as a Goddess.

There are still things I'm working on, always. That's just me. I'm always willing to see the shadow side of myself. I'll still be the first person to raise my hand when I find a class that looks at our shadows. This teaches me how to find what's hidden. That's also how I help you. And I know now that I can handle whatever is hidden. Nothing is too big for me anymore. I have full faith that I can handle everything that presents itself to me. I've got my back. I'm strong enough to do it. I didn't know how strong I was until Tara reminded me.

During this journey, my heart has physically ached at times, and I mistook it for sadness and heartbreak. Now I know it was hurting because it was expanding. It was expanding to give and receive more love. The pain in my heart has been the growth and expansion of everything I set out to do when I started writing this book. Although when I started this journey, I had NO idea of the outcome that would actually present itself. I thought I was going to share a few stories with you and hopefully help you on your own journey. I knew I wanted to share deeper parts of myself with you so you could see there was no shame in what we experience. I got so much more than that.

Even though I wrote this book for you, I quickly learned I really was writing it for myself—so I could learn and know what it is to hold the depths of love, to hold the depths of compassion, and to hold the depths of wisdom, all of which Tara embodies. It's been bringing all these concepts into my body and understanding them on a greater energetic level. I've learned how to love me exactly as I am. Loving me and knowing myself in this way reminds me that you, too, are here to love yourself this way. I have developed an immense amount of compassion for myself and every human being, serving the purpose they came here to serve, just as I am here to serve you. The wisdom in all of this is that everything is already perfect. There is wisdom in allowing our life to unfold in the way it's supposed to. It unfolds in this way when we ask for what we want and know that the way it comes to us is exactly right for us.

We all incarnate here on earth as many times as it takes us to learn the lessons we are here to learn. And I believe before each incarnation on earth, everyone writes their life story. Their soul has already lined up what will unfold and what experiences they need to have in order to feel and heal what they came here to work on. It is unique to every individual. There is no judgment as to the individual life path. It simply is. It's kind of like we've written a movie script before we incarnated, and everyone plays a part in our movie. We play a part in theirs. Every single person around us is affected by our lives, and on the grand scale, we affect every single person by the way we live our lives. Before we incarnate, we choose the roles we will play for everyone significant in our lives. We will dance with each other in these roles as we grow, heal, and release. We all move together.

When we can look at our entire life this way and know we've planned our life as opportunities for growth, it allows for so much expansiveness in our thinking. It allows us to see our life with a floodlight instead of a tiny flashlight. When we choose to see our life from this vantage point, we realize we are always at choice. We can choose to wonder why we are so triggered when someone is allowing themselves to be out in the world, proud of their creations, tooting their own horn.

We can get curious about our own wounds, or we can choose to get critical and judgmental and stay in the quagmire of our own righteousness. We can choose to stay stuck. If we allow the experiences in our life to teach us, then our life is ours. We are no longer at the mercy of someone else. We are the writers of our own story.

From the beginning, I told you I was here to awaken the Divine Feminine, and I am. But now I realize there was more to this journey. I was awakening the Divine Feminine within me first because it was all so deeply buried. I was utterly confused about who she was and how to awaken her. I thought the Divine Feminine was this spiritual, woo-woo concept or devotional practice or ideology that existed outside of me. I believed it would only awaken if I was devoted to a certain path. I didn't realize that I could be devoted to my own journey and be true to myself and it would naturally evolve and awaken within me. I didn't need to be some sort of devotee. It wasn't something that had to happen outside of me. I now understand she manifests through me. I embody her. She is now awake. And I'm getting to know her more every day. I'm listening and learning how she wants to show up with me. I'm honoring my softness. I'm honoring my firmness. I'm honoring my innate knowingness of me.

I know I am safe in this world. It's safe for me to be me. Claiming all of me is one of the reasons I'm here. So I can show you how to do the same. I'm here to show you how to create your own safe space and journey deep within to find what's been hiding, love it, and heal it. This is how we awaken. This is how we liberate ourselves. We learn, we teach, and we guide each other back to ourselves, to the truth that is us. We just need a little encouragement, support, and guidance along the way. Intuitively we already know how to do this; sometimes it gets buried along the way. And when a fellow sister walks this path with us, it makes it all the juicier and more worthwhile.

We awaken to ourselves by accepting us for us, no matter what we've done. When we begin the journey of doing the work that it takes to get this far, we start to love everything about us. And when we finally love everything about us, we have no harsh judgments left for ourselves. And when we have no harsh judgments about ourselves, we have no judgment left to hold against others. It's gone. We get to fully accept others for who they are because we've learned how to fully accept ourselves for who we are with all our continued faults and flaws. We learn to see others with all their flaws and wrongdoings, along with the soul they are here to be, for the child they were, for the woundings they've endured that have filtered the lenses of their lives. We have greater compassion and understanding when we can identify the depths of ourselves in others. This is unconditional love.

Not only have I learned how to love more, I've learned how to allow others to love me more. Up until a few years ago, I had been afraid of letting others fully see me and love me; my heart remained only partially open. Now it's fully open and will continue to stretch and hold more as I do my work in the world.

I've learned how to receive more love. I know that sounds kind of silly: that I've had to learn how to let others love me more. But to allow others to love us, to really, fully, completely love us, we have to be willing to be seen for everything we are—all of our faults and flaws. And that takes work. That's what I've been doing for almost a year. Working!

And because of that, I feel my husband's energy differently now. Recently, I picked him up from the airport. As he was walking toward me, he had a big smile on his face. I could feel something energetically different about him. He gave me a kiss and told me how much he'd missed me. Then he reached out to me and pulled me into him with a slight force. He wrapped his arms around me with an incredible strength I'd never felt before. He was holding me with a different energy than he had ever held me. The hug felt incredible. I loved it.

Shortly thereafter, I started noticing myself becoming irritated with him. I wanted to nitpick at his habits. Then I started to verbalize some of the irritations. I felt sad and confused. I'd already fabricated an argument. Why was I making all his quirks so wrong? He was just as confused about what was going on as I was. Then it occurred to me: a story I'd written over a decade ago while at a writing retreat in Texas.

I was sitting in the sun on a big, heavy stone wall. I journaled about the sun shining on me and how glorious and warm it felt. Then I wrote that for me to be out in the world, shining brightly like the sun, doing the work I'm meant to do, I needed my husband to be as solid as the brick wall I was sitting on. I needed to know that if I was out in the world, doing my work, that he would be solid within himself to hold me. When I wrote this, I wasn't sure exactly what I meant. But I knew I didn't have what I'd just written down.

As I thought about this memory, tears streamed down my cheeks as I realized what had happened with that hug. His engulfing hug at the airport was holding all of me. All the bigness of me that is to be out in the world. I knew in that moment that he could hold all the energy that is me. His arms around me were the most amount of love I've felt. I'd never felt an energetic love like he'd just given me. Maybe he's putting it out the same as he always has, but I feel him in a different way. There's more love, more presence. And I felt his solid grounded strength within himself.

As soon as I put all this together, I realized that I was sabotaging that hug because I was afraid of feeling all that love. I'd never been able to receive love like that from him; it was new to me. It let me know that I can get as big as I need to be, and no matter what that looks like, his energy will still hold me. It's as if the strength with which he can hold me allows me to be free and do everything I'm here to do. I also felt a confirmation of safety to be out in the world. That no matter how far I travel or how long I'm gone, his love will still be here.

Am I the one showing up differently or is it him? Either way, I know this is all because of my growth. And as I've grown, so has he. I know he sees me differently. He's watched me go through this journey of writing a book. Watching someone we love go through such a process brings admiration and adoration. And it's not only been me on this journey; it's also been him. My growth has been his growth.

In addition to awakening the Divine Feminine, I'm also here to awaken humanity. I'm here to liberate us from our shackles. I'm here to remind everyone of their truth and why they came here to this planet. I'm here to awaken you from the sleepy state you've been in. I'm here to shine brightly so you can find me, so I can be a mirror for what you're ready to heal. So you can see yourself through me. So we can hold hands, and you can feel the energy of the Universe flow through your body. I know this to the core of my being. It is firmly rooted in the entirety of me.

Maybe you've seen yourself in my stories. Maybe you've seen yourself in how I began raising my kids. Maybe you identified with my story about my son. Even just identifying with that and seeing yourself in it is a start. You've opened the door. That's huge! Maybe you've already changed some beliefs along the way. Great! Maybe my words and concepts are changing your perspective. Or maybe your spouse had an affair, and you didn't know how to handle it. Maybe you're not proud of the words that came out of your mouth. There's no shame to be had. Know that you were doing the best you could with the knowledge you had of yourself at the time. Love yourself. Have compassion. And when you're ready, take responsibility for your actions.

Looking at our shame and guilt takes courage. It hurts to admit to ourselves where we've fallen short. It also takes bravery to admit to ourselves and those around us that we've been pretending. I was pretending that my life was great and that everything was perfect for more than two decades. Pretending gives us a way forward until we're ready to see our truth. When we're done pretending that we're not hurting ourselves and others by staying silent or keeping things "normal," the light can begin to shine onto our lives. And guess what?! You've already been doing the work.

Celebrate that! Celebrate that you've been allowing yourself to see your shadows; you've allowed yourself to entertain thoughts that you might never have thought you'd entertain. Maybe you've given yourself permission to wonder how life might be different if you start doing it differently. Congratulations! That takes courage. Speaking up for oneself can be nerve-wracking. It might create all kinds of inner turmoil, but know this is the way through. Stepping out of our comfort zones takes tremendous courage. Not everyone does it. Looking at our shadows can be really scary. Looking at the places where we've fallen short of ourselves and our family takes guts. For some of us, it's easier to stay in a place of comfort without change. And if you find yourself there, know that just by reading this book, you've stirred the process.

On each page, you have been awakening to yourself. As you've taken your journey through this book, know that you've unlocked deep places within you. You've opened doors on purpose to release the darkness. You've awakened those parts of yourself that have been waiting to be seen and loved.

That's what this whole book has been about; it's a journey within yourself. Maybe it's to continue something you started long ago, and along the way, life took over, and you forgot yourself. Or maybe this journey within is something you've been wanting to do forever and didn't know how to begin or if you could even handle it. I'm here to tell you that you're stronger than you think you are. You have the power within you to hold this energy for your own healing. You have it! It's always been there.

When you do this work, the energy that you bring to your life is more than you've ever dreamed. It's more than you've been told. You hold a greatness within you that is untapped. Allow it to flow forward. Allow you to flow outward into the world. Be in wonderment and curiosity for what you're here to do.

Divine Beings of the planet, this is your job. To love and uncover the truth of who you are. This is why you are reading and listening to these words. You have followed your calling here. Now continue with your calling. Continue your journey forward. Go have fun. Go be in this embodied expression of who you are, the Divine Feminine Goddess. Go play. Know you are perfection itself and are meant to be here right now. You already are the goddess. You know this to be true. Your path is perfectly paved for this experience. You are your own hero. You're the one you've been waiting for.

I've been channeling an energy that calls itself The Beings of Light for over ten years. At first, it started specifically with clients. I would feel a shift in my body, the energy at the back of my neck and in my ears would shift, my mind would be filled with words and phrases that I don't normally speak, and I would have an overwhelming need to sit in front of my laptop and type these words out. I began typing, and the words that came through were definitely not words that I use on a daily basis. Information came through that I was told was specially and only for an individual. I would transcribe them onto the page exactly as I heard them and then nervously send them off to my clients. Every time I did this, the response was incredible. The words I'd allowed to come through me were exactly what my clients needed. The Beings deliver very specific detailed messages.

As I was finishing up this chapter, I began feeling the familiar energy of a transmission wanting to be channeled. Except this time, there was something slightly different. Now, instead of it being just for a specific person, I knew it was a transmission for everyone. Even though it's a transmission for all who read their words, you will receive exactly what you need to receive from it.

Dear Ones, we are the Beings of Light. We are here to tell you that you are on the path of true forgiveness. You are here to bring the light. You are here to bring love and your own salvation forth. You have thought this was not possible up to this point, and we tell you this is untrue. You are your own savior. You are here to do the work for yourself and for others that come after you. It is you who is here to work, to bring forth the journey for yourself and for others after you to see. You are here to love, to shine the light, to bring forward the glory that is to be on this planet once again.

Your planet was once full of joy and expressions of love. You are here to herald that in once again. There is no mistake, no coincidence you are reading this book right now at this time. Your timing is perfect, Dear One. You are reading these words at the most perfect time for you. You are correct in thinking that this book, these words are perfectly for you. You know everything you've read that resonates with you is exactly for you. All that we tell you, you have been waiting to hear. It is the activation point. You know these words to be true. You feel our words in your body and know them to be truth. They resonate in your cells.

You are here, right now, awakening yourself and awakening those around you. It is your job. You contracted before you came here to this planet to do this job. You signed up with all the other souls here also doing this work. You are all doing this together. Your pods are opening, and you know the work has already started. You are here to continue the process. Do your work. Allow these words, our words and the words of Tara, to open your hearts. To open your minds. To open what is ready to be fully opened. Allow all of these words to flow through your being and awaken the dormant places within you.

You already feel the call. You feel the words doing their work. You feel us talking to you right now, activating this. Dear One, do not doubt that you are already perfect in all your flaws. Do not doubt that you can do this. Do not doubt that this is all for you, that you are capable of achieving your heart's greatest desires. It is completely within you to bring this all forward for yourself.

You already have it within you to bring this about. You just have to do the work. Allow the light to shine upon you, to shine in the darkest areas that you deemed unlovable and unseeable. Allow the light to shine there. Feel its love. Shine the light yourself. Allow these places to heal and release so you may create space, room to bring more love. You can hold the light. You can hold this frequency. You can hold this vibration. The vibration is love. Joy and love are light. This is who you are. This is the truth of you. You are the light, Dear Ones. The Light is you.

We are the Beings of Light, and we bring this information and this vibration to you today for you to begin the journey that you know you are called for. It is the journey of awakening your soul and the soul of others. You are here to do the work yourself and to show others the way. Take your love and your light into the world, Dear Ones. You are ready. You know how to do this. We love you. We are The Beings of Light, and you feel our vibration.

She is here. I am here. We are here.
The awakening is now.

ACKNOWLEDGEMENTS

Writing this book took almost a year, and every day of writing felt like being in therapy. I felt immense highs and deep lows. I dug into the cracks and crevices of the places where I thought I hid all the pain I didn't want to feel. Writing about the shame I'd buried since I was a little girl took love and support and constant reminders that I was on the right path.

Amanda, my book doula, thank you for creating the most sacred container for me to perfectly unfold into this journey. Thank you for intuitively knowing when to push me and when to step back and let the process happen naturally. Thank you for showing me the deeper synchronicities that showed up as we moved through this adventure. For watching me birth more of me as we moved through this process. The power of this book would not be possible without you. I love you!

Sydney, thank you for our Tuesday walks. Thank you for sitting in my office and listening to me process. Thank you for reminding me, all the time, what a great job I was doing. Thank you for using what I was writing and applying it in real-time to your own life so I could see just how powerful this work is. Thank you for witnessing my sob sessions of releasing the pain of remembering. Thank you for sitting with me, even when we didn't say anything. Thank you for always dreaming the bigger picture with me. I love you!

My parents, thank you for the perfection you are for me. I would not have learned the lessons on these pages if you weren't exactly who you were. By you being you, I became me. I love you!

Lynn, I cherish our Monday calls. Thank you for letting me cry through this whole process, mirroring for me what I was birthing, holding space when I was in the middle of the unknown, listening to me, even when I didn't make sense, telling me how proud of me you were, encouraging me every step of this journey. I love you!

Josh, thank you for your amazing work on my body. Each acupuncture session allowed me to move deeper into the process of releasing my pain and my shame. This releasing let me put it all onto the pages of this book. I am in gratitude, every time I walk into your office, for how you tune into what needs to be worked on. Thank you for seeing me. I love you!

Jaime, editor extraordinaire, thank you for seamlessly and effortlessly coming right into our world. Your edits make this process so easy. Thank you for making my words sound even better than they did. I love you!

ACKNOWLEDGEMENTS

Andrea, designer extraordinaire, thank you for your creativity in giving me exactly what I didn't know I wanted in a cover design. I told you about the book and gave you some pictures, and you came back with the beautiful artwork that describes my book perfectly. Thank you for the beautiful layout and asking me about it every step of the way. Who knew there was so much that goes into making a book?! I love you!

And George, love of my life, thank you for every moment you give me to be me, to show up in a fuller version of myself, for loving me through the process of writing a book full of my unhealed trauma, for helping me in ways you don't even know, for providing comic relief exactly when I needed it. I love you!

About the Author

Tara Davis is a multifaceted leader who has dedicated her life to helping others uncover their true potential. With a diverse background as an intuitive life coach, writer, facilitator, and energy healer, Tara brings a unique blend of wisdom and insight to the realm of personal growth and self-discovery.

For years, Tara has guided individuals on transformative journeys of healing and self-realization through her coaching, blog, and podcast and as a retreat facilitator. In *Becoming Tara*, she invites readers to join her on a profoundly personal voyage of transformation, drawing from her own experiences and insights to remember who they truly are.

Tara Davis's mission is to inspire, heal, and guide individuals toward a brighter, more purpose-filled life. To learn more or get in touch, visit www.becomingtara.com.

Made in the USA
Monee, IL
14 January 2024

50828499R10136